CENTRE FOR STUDIES IN SOCIAL SCIENCES, CALCUTTA

R. C. Dutt Lectures on Political Economy, 1993

ECONOMIC LIBERALIZATION IN INDIA

R. C. DUTT LECTURES ON POLITICAL ECONOMY

ASHOK MITRA
Terms of Exchange and Accumulation [1975]

KRISHNA BHARADWAJ
Classical Political Economy and Rise to Dominance of Supply and Demand Theories [1976]

B. N. GANGULI
Some Aspects of Classical Political Economy in the Nineteenth Century Indian Perspective [1977]

I. S. GULATI
International Monetary Development and the Third World : A Proposal to Redress the Balance [1978]

V. M. DANDEKAR
Peasant–Worker Alliance : Its Basis in the Indian Economy [1979]

SUKHAMOY CHAKRAVARTY
Alternative Approaches to a Theory of Economic Growth : Marx, Marshall and Schumpeter [1980]

AMIT BHADURI
Domination, Deterrence and Counterforce : An Analysis of Strategic Objectives and Doctrines in the Superpower Arms Race [1981]

MIHIR RAKSHIT
Trade, Mercantile Capital and Economic Development [1983]

PRABHAT PATNAIK
Time, Inflation and Growth : Some Macroeconomic Themes in an Indian Perspective [1984]

ASHOK RUDRA
Some Problems of Marx's Theory of History [1985]

A. VAIDYANATHAN
India's Agricultural Development in a Regional Perspective [1986]

KANTA RANADIVE
The Political Economy of Poverty [1987]

BALWANTH REDDY
Imperatives of Planned Economic Development [1989]

C. T. KURIEN
On Markets in Economic Theory and Policy [1990]

ECONOMIC LIBERALIZATION IN INDIA

Analytics, Experience and Lessons

DEEPAK NAYYAR

Orient Longman

First Published 1996
Reprinted 1999

Sole Distributors
ORIENT LONGMAN LIMITED

Registered Office
3-6-272 Himayatnagar, Hyderabad 500 029, A.P. (India)

Other Offices
Bangalore, Bhopal, Bhubaneshwar, Calcutta, Chandigarh, Chennai, Ernakulam, Guwahati, Hyderabad, Jaipur, Lucknow, Mumbai, New Delhi, Patna

ISBN 81 250 0860 8

Printed by Swapna Printing Works Pvt. Ltd. Calcutta 700 009 and published by Shiladitya Shome, Registrar, Centre for Studies in Social Sciences, Calcutta, 10 Lake Terrace, Calcutta 700 029

For my students
from whom I have learnt
over the years

Contents

Preface

I WOULD LIKE to thank the Centre for Studies in Social Sciences, Calcutta, for the invitation to deliver the Romesh Chunder Dutt Lectures on Political Economy. It was an honour and a privilege to follow in the footsteps of many eminent scholars. I can only hope that my endeavour conforms to the high standards set by my predecessors.

The aim of this essay, based on my lectures, is to provide an analysis and an assessment of the economic liberalization in India based on theory and experience. The choice of the theme was shaped, in part, by the reality in the national context and the conjuncture in the international context. The significance of the subject, however, extends beyond the reality and the conjuncture. The process of liberalization may affect the living conditions of millions of people. What is more, this attempt at transformation of the economy may have profound implications for polity and society. It is not surprising, then, that there is an intense debate on and a widespread interest in the subject. It is hoped that this essay would stimulate informed debate and contribute to understanding among a much wider readership of concerned citizens.

Some of the ideas developed here have been presented at seminars in India and elsewhere during the past two years. For questions and comments on earlier presentations or preliminary drafts, I would like to thank Amiya Bagchi, Amitava Bose, Nirmal Chandra, Padmanabha Gopinath, Ashok Mitra, Mrituinjoy Mohanty, Rohini Nayyar, Gerry Rodgers, Ignacy Sachs, Srirang Shukla and Lance Taylor. Over this period, I recall questions from my students and conversations with my colleagues at the Centre for Economic Studies and Planning in Jawaharlal Nehru University, which led me to reflect further on the issues. There were, also, perceptive questions from many who had come to the lectures in Calcutta. I am particularly indebted to Amit Bhaduri for helpful discussion and valuable suggestions which clarified many of my ideas on the subject.

New Delhi,
April, 1995

Deepak Nayyar

1. Introduction

As the twentieth century draws to a close, economic liberalization is a buzzword : in distant Latin America, in remote sub-Saharan Africa, in turbulent Eastern Europe and in dynamic but disparate Asia. So much so that structural reform in economies is perceived as both virtue and necessity. In this process, some countries are in search of new models of development, while others are attempting to adapt their erstwhile models of development. India is among the countries that have introduced fundamental changes in their strategy of development in the recent past.

The object of this essay is to provide an analysis and an assessment of economic liberalization in India based on theory and experience. In doing so, I shall consider problems which have arisen in the transition from crisis to stabilization and problems which may arise in the transition from stabilization to growth. I shall also endeavour to analyse the actual or the possible consequences of stabilization, adjustment and reform in the short term, medium term and long term respectively, so as to examine the implications of economic liberalization which would, inevitably, straddle time horizons. It would then be possible to reflect on the lessons that emerge.

The structure of the discussion is as follows. Section 2 considers the origins, the dimensions and the implications of the crisis in the economy which surfaced at the beginning of the 1990s in a longer-term perspective. Section 3 outlines the strategy of macro-economic stabilization combined with fiscal adjustment and structural reform adopted by the government in response to the crisis, setting out its rationale, stating its limitations and highlighting its radical departures from the past. Section 4 discusses the problems of adjustment and transition in terms of economic theory and the actual experience elsewhere. Section 5 examines the evidence on the short-run economic impact of stabilization on inflation, the balance of payments, output, employment and poverty. Section 6 analyses the macro-economics of adjustment in the medium term with reference to the Indian experience. It considers the consequences of adjustment for the possibilities of growth and the distribution of benefits or costs in the economy, as also the implications of the interdependence between stabilization and adjustment, at a macro-level. Section 7 provides a critical evaluation of structural reform in an attempt to explore how economic reforms may or may not influence supply responses. Section 8 situates the process of economic liberalization in India in its wider context and in a longer-term perspective in order to highlight issues which are not, but should be, an integral part of the debate. Section 9 draws together some conclusions that emerge in an attempt to sketch the contours of an alternative view, to introduce correctives and to formulate strategies for the future.

2. The Crisis in the Economy

The external debt crisis which surfaced in early 1991 brought India close to default. The manifestations of this crisis were by no means unusual. Indeed, they reflected the experience of several developing countries a decade earlier. A deep fiscal crisis was juxtaposed with an almost unmanageable balance of payments situation and an acceleration in the rate of inflation. For a foreign exchange constrained economy that always lived a hand-to- mouth existence in terms of external resources and relied on foreign capital inflows at the margin to finance the process of development, a difficult balance of payments situation was nothing new. This time around, however, the problem was both more acute and more complex. For one, the magnitude of the financing need was much larger. For another, the fragile balance of payments situation coincided with, and was partly the outcome of, a deep macro-economic disequilibrium. This crisis in the economy, not attributable to any significant endogenous or exogenous shock, was bound to disrupt the growth process and endanger the price stability.

The origins of the crisis can be traced to the large and persistent macro-economic imbalances during the 1980s. The widening gap between the income and the expenditure of the government led to mounting fiscal deficits which were met by borrowing at home. The steady increase in the difference between the income and the expenditure of the economy as a whole meant persistent current account deficits in the balance of payments, inevitably financed by borrowing from abroad. The internal imbalance in the fiscal situation and the external imbalance in the payments situation were closely related through the absence of prudence in the macro-management of the economy. The macro-economics of this relationship can be reduced to a simple proposition based on the national income accounting identity : *ex post,* the current account deficit in an economy is the sum of (a) the difference between investment and saving in the private sector and (b) the difference between expenditure and income in the government sector.[1] In retrospect, it appears that the government turned this identity into a strategy for the macro-management of the economy during the

1980s. It sought to use the current account deficit in the balance of payments as a means of financing the excess of investment over saving for the economy in general and the excess of expenditure over income for the government in particular. Thus, mounting imbalances in the external sector became a convenient substitute for macro-economic adjustment.

The problems associated with these macro-economic imbalances were sharply accentuated, and perhaps brought forward in time, by the impact of the Gulf crisis on the economy in late 1990. This coincided with an uncertain and disturbed situation in the polity which was followed by a prolonged political interregnum. Taken together, these developments led to an erosion of international confidence in India. Credit ratings in international capital markets plummeted. It is clear, however, that the problems of the economy, which reached crisis proportions in 1991, did not come as a bolt from the blue. They accumulated over several years. The economy was able to cope with and adjust to much larger and more sustained oil shocks in 1973 and 1979. Yet, the minor oil shock of 1990 had a disproportionately large impact because the macro-economic situation was already so fragile.

The fiscal crisis was neither an accident nor a coincidence. It was a direct consequence of the financial profligacy on the part of the government. The gross fiscal deficit of the central government, which measures the difference between revenue receipts plus grants and total expenditure plus net domestic lending, was 8.2 per cent of GDP during the second half of the 1980s, as compared with 6.3 per cent during the first half of the 1980s and 4 per cent in the mid-1970s. This fiscal deficit had to be met by borrowing, mostly from the central bank and the people of India. The consequences emerge clearly from the evidence presented in Table 1. The internal debt of the government accumulated rapidly, rising from 35.6 per cent of GDP at the end of 1980–81 to 53.5 per cent of GDP at the end of 1990–91. The burden of debt servicing also mounted. Interest payments increased from 2 per cent of GDP and 10 per cent of the total central government expenditure in 1980–81 to 4 per cent of GDP and 19 per cent of the total central government expenditure in 1990–91. It is now obvious that any growth process based on such borrowing was simply not sustainable. The underlying fiscal crisis was bound to create a situation where the balance of payments situation would become unmanageable and inflation would exceed the limits of tolerance. The decision makers then, oblivious to criticism, were convinced that they could borrow and spend their way to prosperity. But the inevitable crunch did come.

The balance of payments crisis was neither sudden nor unexpected. It was man-made and policy-induced. The liberalization of the trade regime beginning in the late 1970s and the new regime of industrial policies introduced in the early 1980s taken together created incentives for import-intensive industrialization and increased the import intensity of production.[2] The second half of the 1980s also witnessed a surge in imports for the defence sector. During this period, export performance was at best modest while the growth in remittances tapered off and import substitution in the petroleum sector slowed down. Consequently, the current account deficit doubled from an annual average of $ 2.3 billion or 1.3 per cent

Table 1 *Fiscal imbalances and internal debt of the central government (as a percentage of GDP at market prices)*

Year	Gross fiscal deficit	Revenue deficit	Internal debt	Interest payments	Interest payments as a percentage of central government expenditure
1980-81	6.1	1.5	35.6	2.0	10.0
1981-82	5.4	0.2	35.0	2.0	10.9
1982-83	6.0	0.7	40.1	2.2	11.5
1983-84	6.3	1.2	38.7	2.3	12.4
1984-85	7.5	1.8	42.0	2.6	12.9
1985-86	8.3	2.2	45.5	2.9	13.3
1986-87	9.0	2.7	49.8	3.2	13.5
1987-88	8.1	2.7	51.8	3.4	15.2
1988-89	7.8	2.7	51.7	3.6	16.4
1989-90	7.9	2.6	53.2	3.9	17.4
1990-91	8.4	3.5	53.5	4.0	19.0

Sources : i. For gross fiscal deficit, revenue deficit and internal debt : Reserve Bank of India, *Annual Report, 1991–92.*

ii. For interest payments as a percentage of GDP: Ministry of Finance, *Economic Survey, 1990–91* and *1992–93.*

iii. For interest payments as a proportion of total central government expenditure : Ministry of Finance, *Economic and Functional Classification of the Central Government Budget,* annual issues.

of GDP during the first half of the 1980s to an annual average of $5.5 billion or 2.2 per cent of GDP during the second half of the 1980s. These persistent deficits were inevitably financed by borrowing from abroad. The result was a continuous increase in the external debt which, as Table 2 shows, rose from $ 23.8 billion or 14.3 per cent of

Table 2 *Current account deficits, external debt and debt servicing*

Year	Current account deficit as a percentage of GDP	Medium and Long-term External Debt end-of-year		Debt servicing as a percentage of	
		in US $ million	as a percentage of GDP	Exports	Current Account Receipts
1980-81	1.2	23.8	14.3	14.9	7.9
1981-82	1.4	24.3	14.2	13.5	7.7
1982-83	1.3	27.9	15.6	14.6	8.7
1983-84	1.1	31.1	16.0	17.2	10.3
1984-85	1.2	31.9	17.1	19.8	11.7
1985-86	2.3	37.0	17.4	26.7	15.9
1986-87	2.0	43.8	19.4	39.4	31.0
1987-88	1.9	50.8	19.5	41.3	26.4
1988-89	2.6	53.5	21.1	38.9	25.4
1989-90	2.2	57.7	21.6	31.1	21.5
1990-91	2.3	62.3	23.8	29.8	21.7

Source : i. For current account deficit : Reserve Bank of India, *Report on Currency and Finance*, annual issues.

ii. For medium and long-term external debt : Report of the Economic Advisory Council, *The Current Economic Situation and Priority Areas for Action*, Government of India, New Delhi, December, 1989, P.S-9 (for the period 1980-81 to 1983-84) ; and Reserve Bank of India, *Annual Report 1991-92*, p.214 (for the period 1984-85 to 1990-91).

iii. For debt servicing : *Economic Survey*, annual issues and *Report on Currency and Finance*, annual issues.

Notes : a. The data on medium and long-term external debt reported in Table 2 include external assistance from bilateral or multilateral sources on government account and non-government account, drawings from the IMF, external commercial borrowing and outstanding non-resident deposits.

b. The data on debt servicing in Table 2 are derived from balance of payments statistics as the sum of amortization payments and interest payments. The figures on debt servicing reported by the

Ministry of Finance or the Reserve Bank of India for this period underestimate the burden by a significant proportion because of the incomplete coverage of external debt statistics.

c. The current account deficit–GDP ratios and the external debt–GDP ratios are based on the rupee values of the current account deficit during each fiscal year and the outstanding medium and long-term external debt at the end of each fiscal year, expressed as a percentage of GDP at current market prices (data on GDP are from CSO, *National Accounts Statistics).*

d. The debt-service indicators are based on the rupee value of debt servicing expressed as a percentage of the rupee value of exports and of current account receipts (data on exports and current account receipts are from RBI balance of payment statistics).

GDP at the end of 1980–81 to $ 62.3 billion or 22.8 per cent of GDP at the end of 1990–91.[3] Consequently, the debt service burden also rose from 7.9 per cent of current account receipts and 14.9 per cent of export earnings in 1980–81 to 21.7 per cent of current account receipts and 29.8 per cent of export earnings in 1990–91. These strains, which mounted over the years, stretched to breaking point on account of the Gulf crisis. The balance of payments lurched from one liquidity crisis in mid-January 1991 to another in late-June 1991 and came to the verge of collapse. On both occasions, foreign exchange reserves dropped to levels which were not enough to finance imports even for a fortnight.[4]

The vulnerability of the balance of payments was accentuated by two other factors. First, it became exceedingly difficult to roll over the existing short-term debt in the range of $ 6 billion[5] because of adverse international perceptions of the situation and the overnight borrowing in international capital markets was as much as $ 2 billion. Second, non-resident deposits, where the outstanding amount then was more than $ 10 billion, levelled off in September 1990 with a modest net outflow of $ 0.3 billion in the period October 1990 to March 1991 and a massive net outflow of $ 1.3 billion in the period April 1991 to September 1991[6]. It is clear that if expectations had worsened any further the short-term debt would have been called in and there would have been a run on non-resident deposits.

India thus came close to default. The government was indeed reduced to last-resort measures such as using stocks of gold to obtain foreign exchange, seeking emergency bilateral assistance from donor countries and borrowing under special facilities from multilateral financial institutions. It is obvious that the soft options adopted by the government in the second half of the 1980s claimed their pound of flesh. Instead of introducing real correctives to manage the balance of payments, the short-term debt was incurred mostly to finance imports of petroleum while the non-resident deposits and borrowing in international capital markets were used to sustain import liberalization and defence purchases. External resources were, of course, fungible in use but current account deficits were financed by borrowing of one sort or another. The rapid pile up of external debt and the increased burden of debt servicing ultimately eroded international confidence in India's capacity for repayment.

The price situation also came under mounting pressure. The rate of inflation, in terms of the wholesale price index, climbed from less than 5 per cent in 1985–86 to more than 10 per cent in 1990–91. The evidence presented in Table 3, however, suggests that the price behaviour was not obviously related to monetized deficits, which

Table 3 *Monetized deficits, monetary expansion and inflation*

Year	Monetized deficit as a percentage of GDP	Money supply (M3) percentage growth per annum	Inflation per cent per annum
1980-81	2.6	18.3	17.7
1981-82	2.0	12.8	9.3
1982-83	1.9	16.7	4.9
1983-84	1.9	18.1	7.6
1984-85	2.6	18.9	6.4
1985-86	2.4	15.9	4.5
1986-87	2.4	18.6	5.7
1987-88	2.0	16.0	8.2
1988-89	1.6	21.9	7.5
1989-90	3.0	19.4	7.5
1990-91	2.8	15.1	10.3

Source : Reserve Bank of India, *Annual Report* and *Report on Currency and Finance*, annual issues.

Note : The data on inflation are based on the average-of-period increase in the wholesale price index.

were, on an average, larger than 2 per cent of the GDP, or monetary expansion which was, on an average, about 17 per cent per annum throughout the 1980s.[7] It must be recognized that rates of inflation in India have always been strongly influenced by exogenous shocks such as oil price increases or endogenous shocks such as bad monsoons while real disproportionalities have always been an important underlying factor. At the end of the 1980s, however, when food prices rose in spite of three good monsoons in a row, the build-up of inflationary pressures was also attributable to the large fiscal deficits and an excessive growth in money supply. This liquidity overhang accumulated over several years, in conjunction with structural rigidities and underlying supply–demand imbalances, carried a potential for accelerating inflation.

In retrospect, it is clear that the macro-economic disequilibrium which plunged the economy into a crisis situation was, in a fundamental sense, attributable to the mounting imbalances in the fiscal system. In the 1980s, the fiscal regime shied away from domestic resource mobilization as direct taxes were progressively reduced while indirect taxes, which already contributed the bulk of tax revenues, could not be raised any further because such a step could be inflationary or regressive or both.[8] The inadequate resource mobilization effort was compounded by a profligate increase in public expenditures—whether transfer payments in the form of explicit subsidies or unbridled consumption expenditure—which was driven in part by the competitive politics of populism and in part by the cynical politics of soft options.[9] The problem was accentuated by a spending spree on defence. It is no surprise that the total expenditure outpaced revenue receipts and fiscal deficits grew steadily larger.

The root cause of the fiscal crisis, however, was the revenue expenditure outpacing the revenue receipts. For the central government, the small but consistent revenue surplus of the 1970s was transformed into a revenue deficit which averaged 1.1 per cent of GDP in the period 1980–81 to 1984–85 and 2.6 per cent of GDP in the period 1985–86 to 1989–90[10]. The financing of this revenue deficit through borrowing meant that borrowing was used to support consumption expenditure. Given the existence of capital expenditure on defence and in the social sectors, which did not fetch tangible returns, the rates of return on public investment elsewhere had to be extraordinarily high for it to yield a net income flow to the exchequer. Beyond a point, such a fiscal regime was simply not sustainable. Unfortunately, there were no constraints on the domestic borrowing by the government. In effect, the automatic borrowing from the central bank at low interest rates and the preemptive borrowing from the commercial banking system (based on the high statutory liquidity ratio) at modest interest rates were not subject to any stipulated limits.

At the same time, given India's credit-worthiness and low exposure in international capital markets, direct and indirect borrowing abroad by the government to finance the current account deficit during the 1980s was also relatively easy. In principle, such a process of financing development is sustainable if external resources are used to support investment rather than consumption, provided there is an adequate rate of return on such investments in terms of domestic resources and the economy raises its capacity to transform domestic resources into foreign resources. This should have been possible in an ideal world particularly if, for a given level of domestic savings, the government raised the level of investment by an amount equal to the inflow of external resources. The actual experience in India during the 1980s did not meet most of these conditions. External resources were used in part as a substitute for domestic resources. This was because the fiscal crunch forced the government to finance not just the import costs but also the local costs of investment from these inflows. What is more, external resources were used in part to support consumption and only in part to augment investment. The most obvious example, perhaps, was the use of short-term borrowing to finance imports of petroleum, fertilizers and edible oils in the late 1980s ; the alternative would have been to curb imports or run down reserves. It is also possible that the medium-term borrowing, which provided balance of payments support to sustain the import liberalization, may have created avenues for import-intensive consumption. In either case—whether domestic resources were not mobilized sufficiently for public investment or public expenditure on consumption was not controlled adequately—borrowing abroad became a soft option for the government. It is, therefore, plausible to argue that in the presence of foreign capital inflows, the *actual* public savings were lower than *potential* public savings.[11]

In this context, it is important to stress that the origins of the crisis at the beginning of the 1990s lie in the cavalier macro-management of the economy during the 1980s and not, as claimed by some, in a misplaced strategy of development since the mid-1950s. Given the complexity of the Indian development experience over the past four decades, it would be idle to pretend that everything we did was right but it would be naive to suggest that everything we did was wrong. The reality was a mix of the good, the bad and the indifferent. It would mean too much of a digression to enter into a discussion of these issues here. It is enough to say that there were both successes and failures. In a long-term perspective, the most important achievement was the significant step-up in savings, investment and growth which provided a sharp contrast with the near-stagnation in the colonial era, particularly during the first half of the twentieth century. This was combined with the development of a diversified industrial sector and a sustained expansion in agricultural output which ensured food security, but did not lead to a significant reduction in the absolute poverty. The most important shortcomings, situated in a long-term perspective, were the neglect of human resources, agrarian reform and exports. The declining productivity of investment and the lack of international competitiveness emerged as problems that required a reformulation of policies and a restructuring of the economy.[12] These problems, however, were not simply about resource allocation or relative prices as orthodox economics would have us believe. Resource utilization at a micro-level was a crucial determinant of efficiency just as resource mobilization at a macro-level was a crucial determinant of growth. In my judgement, the shortcomings that persisted in the long run and the problems that emerged in the medium term were both a cause for concern but did not precipitate the crisis in the economy. It was the fiscal mess which began in the early 1980s, the external imbalance which worsened significantly in the second half of the 1980s and the debt crisis which surfaced in the early 1990s, that pushed the economy into an awkward corner. For it is obvious that neither the government nor the country could continue to live beyond its means year after year. Indeed, by early 1991, there was hardly any room for manouevre in living on borrowed money or borrowed time.

3. The Response and the Strategy

In response to the crisis situation, the government set in motion a process of macro-economic stabilization combined with fiscal adjustment and structural reform, not simply to extricate the economy from the mess but also—it is argued by some—to catapult it into a golden age. It needs to be said that this strategy is nothing new. It broadly replicates the response of several developing countries in Latin America and sub-Saharan Africa to the debt crisis in the 1980s which was also guided by IMF programmes of stabilization and World Bank programmes of structural adjustment. Even so, it is necessary to outline the logic and the assumptions of the strategy adopted, as this would enable us to recognize its limitations and highlight the departures from the past.

In any programme of macro-economic stabilization, there are two fundamental objectives. The first object is to preempt a collapse of the balance of payments situation in the short term and to reduce the current account deficit as much as possible. The second object is to curb inflationary pressures and expectations in the short term and to reduce the rate of inflation as soon as possible. Such programmes of stabilization are concerned with the demand side. The time horizon is the short run. The principal instruments of stabilization are fiscal policy and monetary policy, which seek to reduce the level of agregate demand in the economy, often used in conjunction with a devaluation, which seeks to stem destabilizing expectations on the presumption that the problems are attributable to rising fiscal deficits, the associated monetary expansion and an unsustainable exchange rate. This provided the rationale for depreciating the rupee, reducing the fiscal deficit of the government and adopting a tight monetary policy.[13]

It should be recognized that these are the essential components of orthodox stabilization programmes drawn up as part of an arrangement with the IMF. The orthodoxy, however, is based on a set of assumptions that are disputable in terms of economic theory and refutable in terms of actual experience.[14] A reduction in the fiscal deficit may not lead to a corresponding reduction in the current account deficit for the outcome depends on how the reduced absorption at a macro-level is distributed between traded goods and non-traded goods. A monetary squeeze may not reduce rates of inflation if price behaviour is determined by structural rigidities or real disproportionalities. The mode of macro-economic adjustment is by no means certain. In the presence of wage–price rigidities, output adjustments are more likely than price adjustments. Thus the deflation associated with stabilization may lead to a contraction in output rather than a reduction in prices. What is more, in the short run, a substantial devaluation may have an inflationary impact on prices and a contractionary effect on output. The outcome, then, may be stagflation instead of stabilization.

Such questions, however, are about means rather than ends. In a situation of deep macro-economic disequilibrium, stabilization is an imperative. The Indian economy did, in fact, experience two stabilization episodes in response to exogenous shocks which were consequences of oil prices increases during the mid-1970s and in the early 1980s. This time around, however, the crisis was not confined to the balance of payments and stabilization was not dictated by any exogenous or endogenous shock. All the same, the pursuit of stabilization does not represent any departure from the past. On the contrary, it represents an attempted return to prudence in macro-management of the economy which, except for the profligacy in the 1980s, was the rule in independent India.

In response to a debt crisis, stabilization is often combined with adjustment and reform. Such programmes of structural adjustment, based on policy reform advocated by multilateral financial institutions, are concerned with the supply side in an endeavour to raise the rate of growth of output. The time horizon is the medium term. Structural reform seeks to shift resources : (a) from the non-traded goods sector to the traded goods sector and within the latter from import-competing activities to export activities ; and (b) from the government sector to the private sector. Apart from resource allocation, structural reform seeks to improve resource utilization : (a) by increasing the degree of openness of the economy and (b) by changing the structure of incentives and institutions, which would reduce the role of State intervention to rely more on the market place, dismantle controls to rely more on prices and wind down the public sector to rely more on the private sector.

In conformity with the orthodoxy, the government has embarked on a wide ranging reform of the policy regime.[15] Trade policy reform has eliminated most quantitative restrictions on imports except for consumer goods and progressively reduced tariff levels. The desire to increase the degree of openness of the economy extends beyond trade flows to capital flows and technology flows. The liberalization of the regimes for foreign investment and foreign technology is intended to expose domestic firms to international competition further. Industrial policy reform, which has removed barriers to entry for new firms and limits on growth in the size of existing firms, seeks to cut out state intervention in investment decisions. This process is sought to be reinforced by deregulation in the financial sector of the economy so that the allocation and utilization of investible resources is left to the market. Public sector reform is limited so far, but the intention to reduce its role is clear enough.

The underlying presumption is that industrialization based on import substitution and State intervention leads to inefficient resource allocation and resource utilization. Orthodox economic theory in the neo-classical tradition provides the theoretical basis for this approach, but it should be recognized that the analytical construct is narrow. Success at industrialization is not only about resource allocation and resource utilization at a micro-level. It is as much, if not more, about resource mobilization and resource creation at a macro-level. The excessive concern with resource allocation, in terms of static allocative efficiency criteria, and resource utilization, in terms of competition through deregulation and openness, is perhaps misplaced. Significant new developments in the neo-classical tradition whether in industrial economics or in trade theory are almost ignored when such analysis is applied to the problems of industrialization and development. Hence this approach, which is static rather than dynamic in conception, tends to ignore inter-temporal considerations and does not quite incorporate increasing returns, market structures or externalities which are inherent in any process of industrialization. The emphasis on resource allocation or relative prices, in conjunction with a focus on policy regimes or on the cost and the quality of output, is important but disproportionate and serves a limited purpose. For it fails to recognize that policy regimes are permissive rather than causal factors underlying economic performance, which are at best necessary conditions but under no circumstances sufficient conditions in the restructuring of economies.

It is clear that the structural reforms implemented by the government, combined with further reform on the anvil, represent a radical departure from the development strategy of the past four decades. At the same time, it needs to be said that the reform process, which began in the early 1990s, is not India's first experiment with economic liberalization. The first attempt was a shortlived episode of hesitant liberalization in the mid-1960s which coincided with a substantial devaluation of the rupee. The second endeavour came in the late 1970s with a focus on trade liberalization in a comfortable balance of payments situation. The third step was the package of economic policies introduced in the mid-1980s when liberalization of the trade regime gathered momentum and the process of industrial deregulation was set in motion. These liberalization episodes were perceived as correctives for an industrializing economy in transition but did not contemplate any fundamental changes in the objectives or the strategy of development.[16] This time around, however, the changes are significant enough to be characterized as a shift of paradigm.[17]

Any attempt at a broad characterization of the basic departures from the erstwhile strategy of development runs the obvious risk of over-simplification. Yet, it is worth highlighting three dimensions of the contrast between the past and the present. First, the objective function is economic growth combined with economic efficiency. The earlier concern about preventing a concentration of economic power or attempting a redistribution of wealth, never more than rhetoric, has been explicitly abandoned. The objective of bringing about a reduction in poverty and inequality has not been set aside but such concerns about equity have been subsumed in the pursuit of growth on the premise that it is both necessary and sufficient for an improvement in the living conditions of the people. Second, there is a conscious decision to substantively reduce the role of the State in the process of economic development and rely far more on the market. The government will no longer guide the allocation of scarce investible resources, whether directly through industrial licensing or indirectly through intervention in the financial sector. This role will now be performed by market forces. Public investment, it is believed, preempts scarce resources at the expense of private investment and, contrary to what was argued earlier, does not perform the role of a catalyst let alone a leader. The large share of the public sector in investment and output, it is argued, should be progressively reduced because the desire to capture the 'commanding heights' of the economy and the pursuit of a 'socialist pattern' is responsbile for inefficient resource utilization and constitutes a drain on the exchequer. Third, the degree of openness of the economy is being significantly increased and at a rapid pace. The object is not simply to enforce a cost discipline on the supply side through international competition, but also to narrow the difference between domestic and world prices. It is hoped that this would lead to an integration of the structure of production in the domestic economy with the international division of labour in the world economy. Foreign capital and foreign technology are expected to perform a strategic role in the process. Every aspect of this quest for integration with the world economy provides a striking contrast with the strategy of industrialization adopted in post-colonial India.

In sum, the core of the new paradigm is that economic activity should not be guided by physical controls or state intervention. Instead, decisions about investment, production and consumption should be based on relative prices and the market mechanism. What is more, world prices should be the basic determinant of resource allocation. The consequent restructuring of the economy, it is presumed, would impart both efficiency and dynamism to the growth process. Rapid economic growth, it is hoped, would lead to an erdication of absolute poverty.

4. Problems of Transition

In any process of stabilization, adjustment and reform, economies experience problems of transition so that their return to a path of sustained growth combined with price stability is not assured. It is possible to consider such problems of transition at two levels. First, in terms of analysis, we can consider such problems that arise from the interaction between the demand side and the supply side, problems that arise largely on the demand side and problems that arise mostly on the supply side. Second, in terms of actual experience, there are problems which emerge from IMF programmes of stabilization and World Bank programmes of structural adjustment in Latin America and sub-Saharan Africa. The distribution of the burden of adjustment in the process of transition is a problem that surfaces at both levels.

The fundamental problem of transition arises from the fact that the speeds of adjustment on the demand side and on the supply side are considerably different. Fiscal adjustment and monetary discipline can be used to squeeze aggregate demand so that in response to deflation the speed of adjustment on the demand side is fast. The response of demand to expansionary fiscal and monetary policies is just as rapid. On the other hand, the speed of adjustment on the supply side is inevitably slow because resources are not perfectly mobile across sectors or substitutable in uses and prices, particularly of factors, are not completely flexible. This is so even if all the price incentives of a market economy can be brought to function perfectly. The problems are accentuated in economies characterized by structural rigidities which obviously constrain the response to structural reforms. Supply adjustment based on an expansion of output requires structural change through the creation of capacity, alleviation of infrastructural bottlenecks, streamlining of input supplies, reorientation of public utilities and so on, all of which take time. In contrast, supply adjustment based on a contraction of output is, in certain instances, as rapid as demand adjustment. Therefore, the dynamics of demand are fast in both expansion and contraction whereas the dynamics of supply are slow in expansion but faster in contraction. These asymmetries have four macro-economic implications which are crucial in the process of stabilization and adjustment.

First, stabilization policies which are meant to reduce demand may, at the same time, reduce supply even more for the simple reason that a substantial fiscal adjustment and a tight monetary policy squeeze both investible resources and working capital. As the economy contracts from both sides, the current account deficit may possibly be reduced but inflation will not be restrained. Second, in so far as aggregate demand remains greater than aggregate supply, or the sectoral composition of demand does not match the sectoral composition of supply, and balance of payments constraints prevent excess demand from being met through imports, inflation persists. Third, the initial effects of structural reform, particularly where the balance of payments constraint is binding, may lead to a contraction of output in some sectors before an expansion of output in others. This tends to increase the excess demand in the system and exacerbates the problem of inflation. Fourth, fiscal contraction and monetary discipline which squeeze aggregate demand in the short term may constrain supply responses in the medium term. Yet, without a foundation of macro-economic stabilization in the short term, policy reform simply can not produce the desired results in the medium term. This is the crux of the problem when economies begin on adjustment processes in a situation of deep macro-economic disequilibrium.

On the demand side, the optimistic scenario implicit in IMF stabilization programmes is that the inflation would come down and the current account deficit would be reduced, while the economy would adjust at a macro-level through a fall in prices and a rise in the output. This outcome, however, is by no means certain. Nor is the transition from crisis to stabilization. It is not necessary that fiscal austerity and monetary discipline reduce both the current account deficit and the rate of inflation. Reduced fiscal deficits do not always translate into reduced current account deficits if the impact of the consequent deflation is largely on the non-traded goods, so that the reduced domestic absorption may not stimulate exports and dampen imports. A credit squeeze combined with high interest rates does not always curb inflation if inflationary pressures and expectations are influenced not only by excess liquidity but also by real disproportionalities or structural rigidities and if price formation is based on mark-ups, administered-pricing and cost-indexation rather than market-clearing.[18]

The impact of macro-economic adjustment on output from the demand side is also crucial. In principle, an adjustment is possible either through an increase in output or through a decrease in expenditure. In practice, however, economies in crisis are likely to be output-constrained, for if increments in output were easily obtainable countries would not readily forego output and resort to borrowing to meet expenditure. Economic retrenchment, in which countries are forced to cut expenditures, is thus the more probable outcome.[19] This tends to affect output through the aggregate demand and, if there are wage–price rigidities, the mode of macro-economic adjustment may be a reduction in output rather than in prices. At the same time, a significant devaluation, which is often an integral part of stabilization programmes, may exacerbate the rise in prices and reinforce the contraction in output at least in the short run. Devaluations escalate inflation directly through cost-push and indirectly through mark-ups. The consequent cut in real wages, and the possible deterioration in the terms of trade following a devaluation, may reduce real income in the economy, leading to a contractionary effect on the output.[20]

It would appear that the transition path to stabilization is like walking a tightrope. If inflation does not slow down or the balance of payments does not stabilize, the intended virtuous circle is easily transformed into an unintended vicious circle as the exchange rate and the price level chase each other. In these situations, particularly where the mode of macro-economic adjustment is a contraction of output, stagflation is a probable scenario.[21]

On the supply side, the optimistic scenario implicit in liberalization programmes guided by the Bretton Woods institutions is that structural reform would impart both efficiency and dynamism to the growth process in the medium term. The transition from stabilization to growth, however, is by no means assured. The sequence and the pace of restructuring must be such that it can be absorbed by the economy. If this is not the case, things can go wrong. Trade policy reform may stimulate output by creating economic efficiency gains, but it can also move an economy from a situation of too much protection to a situation of too little protection and, if the manufacturing sector is unable to cope with such a rapid transition, the outcome may be forced deindustrialization. Industrial deregulation which removes barriers to entry and limits on growth may increase competition among firms and improve resource utilization. But it often leads to retrenchment or closures and cannot wish away barriers to exit particularly in economies where levels of income are low, levels of unemployment are high and social safety nets are absent. Deregulation in the financial sector, unless it is paced with care, can be perilous not just in terms of bubbles that burst or scandals that surface, but also if it diverts scarce resources from productive uses into speculative activities. Public sector reform, which is based on a sale of government assets and rudimentary forms of privatization, may not resolve the real problems of efficiency or productivity but can end up socializing the costs and privatizing the benefits. Therefore, the content, the sequence and the speed of policy reform must be planned and calibrated in a careful manner, such that it recognizes structural rigidities where they exist instead of assuming structural flexibilities where they do not exist.

There is also a mismatch between the simplicity of orthodox theory and the complexity of diverse reality which should be recognized. The discipline of the market may not suffice to ensure efficiency in terms of resource utilization because the economic organization of production at a micro-level is not simply about the presence or absence of price competition. Similarly, getting prices right may not have the desired effect in terms of resource allocation because resources are neither as flexible in price nor as substitutable in use as neo-classical economics suggests. The restructuring of economies on the supply side, then, is easier said than done, for supply responses may be induced but cannot be assured by policy regimes alone. In sum, problems of transition are a reality that cannot be wished away.

The actual experience of stabilization, adjustment and reform programmes in Latin America and sub-Saharan Africa, guided by the IMF and the World Bank in a medium-term perspective, also reflects problems of transition. The critical evaluation of these programmes in the literature on the subject points to significant dangers.[22] First, almost without exception, there is an adverse impact on poverty in so far as the burden of adjustment is borne largely by the poor. Second, these programmes tend to stifle long-term growth prospects so that a return to the path of sustained growth is often a hope rather than a reality. Third, such programmes tend to over-estimate export prospects and the availability of external finance. And when this does not materialize, economies are forced into a deflation that imposes social costs and squeezes supply responses. Fourth, there is a steady externalization of policy formulation. For one, responsiveness to changing and evolving situations is significantly reduced as policy prescriptions are characterized by an analytical absolutism : if you have a balance of payments problem the answer lies in liberalizing trade and if you have a fiscal crisis the answer lies in reducing tax rates. For another, sensitivity to social and political realities is sharply eroded as national policies are shaped without reference to the context.[23] In evaluating the experience across countries, it is difficult to define and then identify 'success' or 'failure' because actual outcomes span a wide spectrum from moderate successes at one end to real disasters at the other. But the diverse experiences do establish that the transitions from crisis to stabilization and from stabilization to growth are characterized by a discernible set of problems.

Macro-economic adjustment and structural reform are not simply a matter for academic analysis or intellectual concern. In the period of transition, these processes impose a burden of adjustment that is distributed in an asymmetric manner. Without correctives, the burden of adjustment is inevitably borne by the poor. For all the rhetoric about social safety nets, economies in crisis simply do not have the resources for this purpose. It cannot suffice to assert, as governments often do, that the burden of such adjustment would have to be borne by the affluent simply because it is the rich who have the incomes to immunize themselves from the burdens of structural change. It is obvious that there can be no adjustment without pain. But pain for whom ? Surely, in keeping with the equity principle, the costs must be borne by those who enjoyed the pleasures derived from profligacy. Reality turns out to be the opposite. Inflation tends to make the rich better off as it redistributes incomes from wages to profits and the poor worse off as it erodes their incomes which are not index-linked. The soft options in fiscal adjustment tend to squeeze public expenditure in social sectors where there are no vocal political constituencies, as the resources allocated for poverty alleviation, health care, education and welfare programmes decline in real terms. Restructuring on the supply side, which follows structural reform, inevitably imposes a burden on wage labour. Such outcomes, borne out by evidence available, can only hurt the poor.[24] Adjustment with a human face is then an illusion.

5. The Stabilization Experience

The process of macro-economic stabilization was initiated in mid-1991. The period since then is long enough to attempt an assessment. There are two important questions that arise. First, what is the evidence on the stabilization experience in terms of restraining inflation and managing the balance of payments situation ? Second, what is the economic impact of stabilization on growth, employment and poverty in the short term ?

Table 4 *Annual rates of inflation : 1989-90 to 1994-95*

(Point-to-point)

	1989-90	1990-91	1991-92	1992-93	1993-94	1994-95
Wholesale price index	9.1	12.1	13.6	7.0	10.8	10.4
Consumer price index for industrial workers	6.6	13.6	13.9	6.1	9.9	9.7
Consumer price index for urban non-manual employees	8.0	13.4	13.6	6.8	8.3	9.9
Consumer price index for agricultural labourers	1.0	16.6	21.9	0.7	11.6	10.6

(Average-of-period)

	1989-90	1990-91	1991-92	1992-93	1993-94	1994-95
Wholesale price index	7.5	10.3	13.7	10.0	8.4	10.8
Consumer price index for industrial workers	6.6	11.2	13.5	9.9	7.3	10.3
Consumer price index for urban non-manual employees	6.9	11.0	13.7	10.5	6.9	9.5
Consumer price index for agricultural labourers	5.4	7.6	19.3	12.4	3.5	11.9

Sources: i. Office of the Economic Adviser, Ministry of Industry : for wholesale price index ;

ii. Labour Bureau : for consumer price indices for industrial workers and agricultural labourers ;

iii. CSO : for consumer price index for urban non-manual employees.

A. Inflation

The facts on inflation are clear enough. Table 4 sets out the annual rates of inflation in terms of the wholesale price index and the consumer price indices. It shows that there was a discernible increase in the rate of inflation in 1991–92, irrespective of how we measure it, which was followed by some deceleration in inflation on a point-to-point basis in 1992–93 and on an average-of-period basis in 1993–94. But the rate of inflation gathered momentum once again thereafter. The evidence available does not suggest a real turn-around during the period of stabilization, for inflation remained in the range of 10 per cent per annum. This can be described as a success only if Latin American economies are our point of reference. It is close to a failure if India's past record is the norm. Indeed, the five years from 1990–91 to 1994–95 is the longest period of sustained double-digit inflation in independent India. This persistent inflation during the first half of the 1990s is somewhat puzzling. For one, it has coincided, for most of the time, with a concerted attempt at stablization. For another, it has coincided, entirely, with five good monsoons in a row. What is more, the economy has not experienced any significant exogenous shock over this period.

The factors underlying this price behaviour merit scrutiny. The government claims that its stabilization policies have played an important if not leading role in arresting inflation. It is not clear how. Indeed, these policies almost certainly accentuated inflation during 1991–92 and probably contributed to it in subsequent years. In principle, the substantial fiscal adjustment together with the tight monetary policy should have led to a contraction of aggregate demand and thus dampened demand-pull inflation. However, the impact may have been reduced in so far as the real disproportionalities underlying the inflationary pressures persisted. But that is not all. The nature of the fiscal adjustment in the stabilization programme was bound to fuel cost-push inflation when subsidies were cut as on fertilizers, administered prices were raised as for petroleum products, or user-charges were hiked by public utilities as for electricity. The tariff reform, which reduced customs duties across the board, was sought to be made revenue-neutral not through an increase in direct taxes that would reduce disposable incomes of the rich and dampen inflation but through increases in excise duties that would fuel inflation and squeeze real incomes of the poor. The substantial depreciation of the rupee, explicit in the exchange rate adjustments and implicit in the so-called partial convertibility or full convertibility, obviously contributed to the inflation by raising the cost of imported intermediates and the mark-ups on final goods. In the sphere of monetary policy, the liquidity overhang inherited from the past and the parallel economy were always beyond the reach of discipline. However, it appears that monetary policy was also somewhat lax for the increase in money supply, defined as M3, was about 18 per cent per annum from 1991–92 to 1994–95, which was not significantly lower than the unbridled monetary expansion of the 1980s.[25] Although liquidity was not tight enough to reduce demand-pull inflation, the high interest rates, which have been a part of the stabilization programme, did probably contribute to cost-push inflation.

In my judgement, the rate of inflation would have been higher than what it was, were it not for the succession of good monsoons, and, in particular, the bumper harvest in 1992–93. The reason is simple. In the absence of exogenous shocks, the performance of the agricultural sector has always been the crucial determinant of price behaviour in India. Bad harvests fuel inflation and good harvests dampen it.[26] Food prices, in particular, lead the general price level and influence inflationary expectations. In this context, it is worth noting that the bounty of the weather gods may have been neutralized, in part, by stabilization policies. The sharp reduction in fertilizer subsidies, reinforced by a politics of compromise, led to a more than compensatory increase in the procurement prices of foodgrains. The objective of restraining food subsidies led to a sharp increase in the issue prices of foodgrains in the public distribution system. Consequently, the procurement prices of common paddy and wheat were both raised by more than 50 per cent between 1990–91 and 1993–94. At the same time, the issue prices in the public distribution system were raised even more, by 86 per cent for common rice and by 72 per cent for wheat, between mid-1990 and early 1994.[27] These increases exercised an important influence on market prices of foodgrains and, in turn, on inflation.

B. Balance of payments

The balance of payments situation, it would seem, has been transformed. The capital outflow from the repatriable deposits held by non-resident Indians, which assumed massive proportions during the first half of 1991–92, came to a stop. The exposure in terms of short-term debt was reduced from $ 6 billion at the end of 1990–91 to $ 1.8 billion at the end of 1993–94. The level of foreign exchange reserves climbed from a meagre $ 2.2 billion in end-March 1991 to $ 5.6 billion in end-March 1992, increased slowly to $ 6.4 billion in end-march 1993 and rose further to a comfortable $ 15.1 billion in end-March 1994. The stoppage of capital flight, the reduction in the short-term debt and the accumulation of foreign exchange reserves provide evidence of stabilization. But an analysis of the available evidence on the nature of balance of payments adjustment (presented in Table 5) and on the composition of capital inflows which met the financing need (set out in Table 6), suggests that this process of stabilization is certainly not complete and possibly not sustainable.

The adjustment in the balance of payments, during the period from 1991–92 to 1993–94, was based on a substantial reduction in the balance of trade deficit not only in terms of dollar values but also as a proportion of GDP. The associated reduction in the current account deficit was greater. Much of this adjustment, however, was attributable to import contraction rather than export expansion. Even though the petroleum import bill did not register any significant decline, the dollar value of total imports, throughout this period, remained lower than it was in 1990–91. The slump in non-oil imports was a consequence of the draconian import compression in 1991–92 and the sluggishness of import demand thereafter. At the same time, except for the spurt in 1993–94, there was a stagnation in the dollar value of exports.

The smaller current account deficits, which reduced the financing need, combined with capital inflows were responsible for the build-up of reserves. But financing was not available from the usual sources such as external assistance where net resource inflows continued to decline, or commercial borrowing where access to international capital markets was virtually closed. It is possible to distinguish between three sets of extraordinary capital flows, the exact magnitudes of which are reported in Table 6, as the main sources of external finance. The first set was constituted by borrowing from the IMF, structural adjustment loans from the World Bank or the Asian Development Bank and special bilateral assistance from donor countries. Taken together, such exceptional financing provided $ 2.2 billion in 1991–92, $ 2.4 billion in 1992–93 and $ 1.2 billion in 1993–94. The second set was made up of capital

Table 5 *Balance of payments adjustment : 1989-90 to 1993-94*

(In US $ million)

	1989-90	1990-91	1991-92	1992-93	1993-94
Foreign exchange reserves end-of-year	3368	2236	5631	6434	15068
Net inflows (+) or outflows (−)					
Non-resident deposits (FCNR and NRER Accounts)	+1475	+252	−1638	+125	−1637
Exports	16626	18143	17866	18537	22173
Imports	21272	24073	19411	21882	23212
of which :					
Oil	3768	6028	5364	6100	5756
Non-oil	17504	18045	14047	15782	17456
Balance of trade deficit	4646	5930	1545	3305	1039
Current account deficit	7269	8424	2135	3603	315
Extraordinary capital inflows (excluding external assistance and commercial borrowing)	–	2547	4938	4031	7886

(In US $ billion)

	1989-90	1990-91	1991-92	1992-93	1993-94
External debt	62.8	68.4	73.4	77.5	78.7
of which :					
Short term	5.5	6.0	5.6	4.5	1.8
Medium and long term	57.3	62.4	67.8	73.0	76.9
(Memorandum item : Rupee debt)	(11.0)	(12.8)	(10.4)	(10.6)	(10.1)

(As a percentage of GDP)

	1989-90	1990-91	1991-92	1992-93	1993-94
Exports	6.1	6.1	7.2	7.6	8.8
Imports	7.8	8.1	7.8	9.0	9.3
of which :					
Oil	1.4	2.0	2.1	2.4	2.3
Non-oil	6.4	6.1	5.7	6.6	7.0
Balance of trade deficit	1.7	2.0	0.6	1.4	0.5
Current account deficit	2.7	3.2	0.8	2.2	0.1
External Debt	23.6	24.9	35.1	34.4	31.4

(Percentages)

	1989-90	1990-91	1991-92	1992-93	1993-94
External debt/exports	389.2	408.0	490.8	450.5	354.5
Debt servicing/exports	39.4	38.8	39.9	41.9	34.1

Sources : i. For foreign exchange reserves, net inflows/outflows in non-resident deposits and current account deficit : Reserve Bank of India, *Annual Reports* and Ministry of Finance, *Economic Survey* annual.

ii. For exports, imports (oil and non-oil) and balance of trade : Directorate General of Commercial Intelligence and Statistics, Calcutta.

iii .For external debt : Reserve Bank of India, *Annual Report, 1993–94,* pp. 237-9.

iv. For debtservicing : Ministry of Finance, *India's External Debt : A status Report,* New Delhi, October 1993, P.7 and *Economic Survey, 1994-95.*

v. For extraordinary capital flows, see Table 6.

Notes : a. The statistics on external debt in this table are based on a new definition and classification which is exhaustive and are thus not comparable with those in Table 2. The are two main differences. First, in the new definition, medium and long-term debt includes government and non-government borrowing from multilateral and bilateral sources, drawings from the IMF, external commercial borrowing, outstanding non-resident deposits including interest credited to these accounts, foreign currency deposits by banks and others from abroad, export credit of maturity longer than one year and borrowing for defence purchases. Second, in the new definition, all short-term debt is included. Unfortunately, data based on the new definition and classification of external debt are available only from 1989–90 and not for the earlier period. There are, however, two exclusions from external debt in Table 5. First, the rouble debt (civilian and defence) to the erstwhile USSR, now denominated in rupees and repayable in exports to Russia, is excluded ; this is because it represents an accumulated debt from the past which has not changed in the period under review, but its US dollar equivalent, at current exchange rates, is set out in parentheses as a memorandum item. Second, short-term debt with a maturity of six months or less (which was in the range of $ 2 billion throughout this period) is excluded ; this is in accordance with the normal reporting practice in debt statistics.

b. The figures on exports, imports, balance of trade, current account deficit and external debt as a percentage of GDP have been calculated from the respective rupee values at current exchange rates and CSO data on GDP at current market prices.

c. The debt-service indicators are also calculated as percentages from the respective rupee values at current exchange rates. Debt servicing payments on the rupee debt to the USSR/Russia are excluded from these proportions.

flows that originated in non-residents. The amnesties announced by the government raised $ 2.2 billion in 1991–92, largely in the form of borrowing from non-residents through bonds and partly through

Table 6 *Capital flows to meet financing needs in the balance of payments : 1990–91 to 1993–94 (in US $ million)*

	1990-91	1991-92	1992-93	1993-94
IMF (gross drawals)	1858	1240	1623	325
Exceptional financing : (Structural/sectoral adjustment loans from the World Bank and ADB and special bilateral assistance)	–	1000	826	851
Amnesties				
India Development Bonds	–	1373	189	–
Remittances	–	863	–	–
Special deposits				
Special bonds for non-residents	262	–	–	–
Foreign currency (banks and others) deposits	262	304	350	−576
Foreign currency non-resident (banks) scheme	–	–	–	1075
Non-resident (non-repatriable) rupee deposit scheme	–	–	610	1187
Foreign investment				
Direct investment	165	150	341	620
Portfolio investment	–	8	92	3490
Foreign currency convertible bonds	–	–	–	914
Total	2547	4938	4031	7886
Increase (+)/decrease (−) in foreign exchange reserves during the year	−1132	+3395	+803	+8634

Source : Reserve Bank of India, *Annual Report, 1991-92,* p.71 ; *Annual Report, 1992-93,* p.78 and p.226 and *Annual Report, 1993-94,* p.86, p.96 and p.97.

remittances.[28] Special deposits, of one sort or another, brought in $ 1 billion in 1992–93 and $ 2.2 billion in 1993–94.[29] The third set comprised of private foreign capital inflows. Direct foreign investment, which was not new, provided just $ 0.3 billion in 1992–93 and a modest $ 0.6 billion in 1993–94 while portfolio investment, altogether new in India, contributed as much as $ 3.5 billion in 1993–94. These extraordinary capital flows obviously met the financing need earlier, particularly in 1990–91, but also accounted for much of the accumulation in foreign exchange reserves in the subsequent years. The close correspondence between the sum total of these capital inflows and the movements in reserves, particularly in 1991–92 and 1993–94, which emerges from the data in Table 6, is striking.

It is clear that the extraordinary capital flows in the form of borrowing from multilateral financial institutions or from non-residents through amnesties and special deposits are once-and-for-all in nature and cannot provide a sustained access to external resources. What is more, except for remittances in the amnesty scheme and the principal in the rupee deposit scheme, all of this constituted borrowing abroad to support the balance of payments which led to a rapid accumulation of external debt. Consequently, between end-March 1991 and end-March 1994, the outstanding medium and long-term debt increased by $ 14.5 billion, while total external debt rose from less than one-fourth of the GDP at the end of 1990–91 to about one-third of the GDP during the period of stabilization from 1991–92 to 1993–94. It is not surprising that there was a corresponding deterioration in the ratio of outstanding debt to total exports. The proportion of export earnings preempted by debt servicing was as high as 40 per cent. Although foreign investment represented non-debt-creating capital flows, the share of direct investment was small while that of portfolio investment was large. Recent experience from elsewhere suggests that the sustainability and the stability of such portfolio investment inflows is open to question for it is strongly influenced by confidence and expectations.

In sum, it seems that the level of foreign exchange reserves remains comfortable despite the modest export performance essentially because of the sluggishness of import demand on the one hand and the substantial external borrowing and now portfolio investment on the other. The process of stabilization would not be complete unless the export surge is maintained and the balance of trade situation improves even after import demand revives. The process of stabilization may not be sustainable in so far as the build-up of reserves is based on a further accumulation of external debt. A reliance on capital flows that are once-and-for-all or volatile in nature cannot stabilize the balance of payments.

In this context, it is worth noting that the comfort implicit in the size of reserves may be illusory in so far as these foreign currency assets are more than matched by foreign exchange liabilities which have short maturities or can be withdrawn on demand. Consider, for example, the situation in end-March 1994.[30] The level of foreign exchange reserves was $ 15.1 billion. Short-term debt with a maturity of six months, or less, was $ 1.8 billion. Short-term debt with a maturity of more than six months, upto one year, was another $ 1.8 billion. The par value of outstanding portfolio investment, without allowing for capital gains realizable and repatriable, was $ 3.5 billion. These short-term liabilities in foreign exchange added up to $ 7.1 billion which was the equivalent of almost 50 per cent of the foreign exchange reserves. But that is not all. The outstanding stock of repatriable deposits held in India, mostly by non-residents but partly by foreign entities, with a maturity of more than one year and upto three years, was as much as $ 12.7 billion. It must be recognized that such deposits can be withdrawn on demand and, recent experience confirms, are susceptible to capital flight should there be any crisis of confidence. Thus, at the end of the fiscal year 1993–94, the total liabilities, which could be called in at short notice, were $ 19.8 billion compared with reserves of $ 15.1 billion. Available evidence does not suggest any qualitative change in the situation during 1994–95.[31]

C. Growth and employment

The short-term impact of macro-economic adjustment on output and growth is almost always adverse. The stabilization experience in India so far is no exception. Table 7 sets out the evidence on sectoral growth rates in output as also the growth in GDP at constant prices between 1989–90 and 1993–94. It shows that, in real terms, GDP growth was 1.1 per cent in 1991–92, 4 per cent in 1992–93 and 4.3 per cent in 1993–94. These trends are, in part, attributable to the performance of the agricultural sector, poor in 1991–92, robust in 1992–93 and good in 1993–94, which was a consequence of the monsoon factor rather than stabilization policies. But the deflation implicit in aggregate demand management also had its impact as the government reduced fiscal deficits, contracted real expenditures and tightened monetary policy. Consequently, industrial output dropped by 1.7 per cent in 1991–92, rose by 2.6 per cent in 1992–93 and increased by 3.9 per cent in 1993–94. The decline in the

Table 7 *Sectoral growth rates at constant prices : 1989–90 to 1993–94 (per cent per annum)*

	1989–90	1990–91	1991–92	1992–93	1993–94
GDP at factor cost	6.9	4.9	1.1	4.0	4.3
Agriculture, forestry and fishing	1.7	3.8	– 2.5	5.0	2.9
of which agriculture	1.1	4.1	– 2.7	5.3	3.0
Industry	11.6	6.3	– 1.7	2.6	3.9
of which manufacturing	11.7	6.2	– 3.2	2.0	3.6
Services	8.5	4.6	5.3	4.1	5.4

Source : CSO, *National Accounts Statistics,* August, 1994 (for 1989–90 to 1992–93) and *Quick Estimates of National Income,* February, 1995 (for 1993–94).

Note : The data for 1992–93 are provisional while the data for 1993–94 are quick estimates.

manufacturing output was much more whereas the revival was somewhat less. These developments provide a sharp contrast with the trend rates of growth through the 1980s.

In the absence of concrete evidence, it is only possible to sketch a plausible hypothesis about the impact of this slow-down in growth on employment. It is reasonable to presume that growth in employment in the agricultural sector was not affected much in so far as the increase in output was sustained, entirely because of the sequence of good monsoons and possibly despite the stabilization policies. In contrast, it is most likely that growth in employment in the industrial sector was dampened by the near-stagnation in the output.[32] The contraction in public expenditure and the recession in the industrial sector, associated with stabilization, must have had an adverse effect on rural non-agricultural employment and urban informal sector employment given the flexibility of labour markets in such employment. In this context, it is important to recognize that the growth of the labour force in India has always been higher than the growth of employment.[33] What is more, the already low employment elasticities registered a significant decline over the past two decades.[34] Under the circumstances, it is almost certain that both underemployment and open unemployment increased at a more rapid pace during the period of stabilization. It is plausible to argue, though impossible to prove, that landless labourers in the rural sector and casual wage labour in the urban sector were probably the most affected by the increasing underemployment and unemployment.

D. Poverty

The probable increase in unemployment among the vulnerable sections of the population during the period of stabilization coincided with a definite increase in food prices. It would be reasonable to infer that this led to an increase in the incidence of poverty in both rural and urban India. The database for poverty estimates is provided by National Sample Survey tables on consumer expenditure, but these are now compiled only on a quinquennial basis and the last such round was conducted for 1987–88. The National Sample Survey does, however, collect data on consumer expenditure by decile groups on an annual basis. But this is based on thin samples. It is, therefore, not comparable with the quinquennial rounds in terms of either coverage or reliability. All the same, it is better than mere inference or assertion. Estimates of the proportion and the number living below the poverty line, based on these thin samples, are presented in Table 8. It reveals that, between 1989–90 and 1992–93, the proportion of the population living below the poverty line increased from 34 per cent to 41 per cent while the number of persons living below the poverty line rose from 282 million to 355 million. The increase was far more pronounced in rural India than it was in urban India. This trend provides a sharp contrast with the steady reduction in the percentage of the population below the poverty line over the period from 1973–74 to 1987–88.[35]

There can be little doubt that the major factor underlying this increase in the incidence of poverty was the rapid increase in food prices. The available evidence on trends in the prices of food as also on some contributory factors, during the period from 1989–90 to 1994–95, is set out in Table 9. It shows the persistence of inflation in the prices of foodgrains despite the succession of good monsoons, induced perhaps by the substantial increases in the procurement prices for producers and a more than commensurate increase in the public distribution system prices for consumers. The pressure on prices may have been accentuated, at the margin, by the trade

Table 8 *Estimates of poverty in India : 1989–90 to 1992–93*

Year	1989–90	1990–91	1991–92	1992–93
Proportion below the poverty line (percentages)				
Rural	33.7	35.0	40.0	41.7
Urban	36.0	37.0	37.6	37.8
Total	34.3	35.5	39.4	40.7
Number below the poverty line (million)				
Rural	206.7	218.4	255.6	269.0
Urban	75.1	79.5	81.6	85.8
Total	281.8	297.9	337.2	354.8

Source : National Sample Survey and Gupta (1994).

Note : These estimates of poverty are based on the methodology suggested by the Expert Group on Estimation of Proportion and Number of Poor (Planning Commission, 1993). The poverty line associated with a calorie intake of 2400 calories per capita per day in rural areas and 2100 calories per capita per day in urban areas was estimated for 1973–74 : Rs. 49.09 per capita per month in rural India and Rs. 56.64 per capita per month in urban India. The poverty lines for subsequent years have been constructed using the consumer price index for agricultural labourers for rural areas and a simple average of the consumer price index for industrial workers and the consumer price index for urban non-manual employees for urban areas as deflators.

liberalization which relaxed or removed quantitative restrictions on exports of agricultural commodities.[36] The evidence presented in Table 9 confirms that there was a discernible increase in the exports of food grains. These exports were, of course, very small as a proportion of the total output but were somewhat larger as a proportion of the marketed surplus, particularly for rice, and thus significant enough to exercise some influence on domestic prices. The increase in food prices was juxtaposed with a stagnation and decline in the per capita availability of foodgrains. What is worse, over this period, there was no discernible increase in the allocation for the public distribution system while the sales through the public distribution system declined steadily as the difference between ration-shop prices and market prices narrowed to a small margin.[37] Ironically enough, there was a steady accumulation in the stock of foodgrains. It would seem

Table 9 *Foodgrains prices and some underlying factors*

Year	1989–90	1990–91	1991–92	1992–93	1993–94	1994–95
Wholesale price index point-to-point increase (per cent per annum)	– 3.6	22.5	24.0	– 1.6	17.4	8.6
Procurement prices (rupees per quintal)						
Paddy (common)	185	205	230	270	310	340
Wheat	215	225	275	330	350	360
Public distribution system central issue prices (rupees per quintal)						
Rice (common)	244	289	377	437	537	537
Wheat	204	234	280	330	402	402
Per capita availability (grams per day)						
Cereals	453	435	468	434	427	436
Pulses	42	41	42	34	37	38
Exports (thousand tonnes)						
Rice	422	527	678	580	805	891
Wheat	12	134	587	37	1	58
Coarse cereals	6	7	14	17	194	69
Pulses				34	43	59

Source : Ministry of Finance, *Economic Survey, 1993-94* and *1994-95.* For data on exports, Directorate General of Commercial Intelligence and Statistics, Calcutta.

Notes : a. Procurement prices relate to crop years.
b. Estimates of per capita availability relate to calendar years.

that the higher procurement prices for producers enabled the government to add to its stockpile of food but the higher issue prices for consumers meant that these inventories could not be utilized so that the public distribution system failed to serve its intended purpose. The price of food, not only in the market place but also in the ration shops, was simply too high for the poor.

But that is not all. The inflation was just as high in other food articles and food products. This emerges clearly from the data in

Table 10 *Rates of inflation in necessities (point-to-point : per cent per annum)*

Commodity group	Weight (%)	1989-90	1990-91	1991-92	1992-93	1993-94	1994-95
Food articles (wholesale price index)	17.39	1.7	19.2	20.9	5.5	4.4	11.9
Food products (wholesale price index)	10.14	13.4	13.0	9.9	16.2	12.3	8.1
Essential commodities							
Wholesale price index	21.77	n.a.	13.6	15.8	4.8	12.0	10.0
Consumer price index	48.83	n.a.	14.7	15.7	3.0	12.1	10.4

Source : Ministry of Finance, *Economic Survey, 1992-93, 1993-94* and *1994-95.*

Note : The price indices for essential commodities are compiled by the Ministry of Finance from the WPI and CPI (IW) index numbers.

Table 10. Indeed, the basket of essential commodities experienced double digit inflation throughout, except in 1992–93, in terms of both the wholesale price index and the consumer price index. Consequently, between end-March 1990 and end-March 1995, the prices of foodgrains rose by 90 per cent, the prices of primary food articles rose by 77 per cent and the prices of manufactured food products rose by 62 per cent.[38] Given such inflation in food and in the prices of necessities, it would not be surprising if the incidence of poverty registered a further increase in 1993–94 and 1994–95. In this context, it is worth noting that the purchasing power of the poeple, even as an arithmetic average, did not register any increase during the period of stabilization. In real terms, both per capita national income and per capita private final consumer expenditure in the domestic market experienced a stagnation or decline.[39] It is, then, plausible to argue that the inflation, which was concentrated in the prices of wage goods, probably redistributed incomes away from the poor leaving them worse off.

6. Macro-Economics of Adjustment

THE PRECEDING discussion has sought to focus on the short-term impact of stabilization at a macro-level. Let me now consider the medium-term consequences and implications. In doing so, I shall explore two sets of questions. For one, what is the impact of stabilization and adjustment on the possibilities of growth and the distribution of benefits or costs in the economy? For another, what are the macro–economic implications of the interaction between stabilization and adjustment which straddles time horizons?

A. *Quality of adjustment*

In my judgement, the quality of fiscal adjustment in the government sector, which constitutes the core of macro-economic adjustment, leaves much to be desired particularly when situated in a medium-term perspective. There are three reasons underlying my concern : (a) it cannot provide a sustainable solution to the fiscal crisis; (b) it is likely to constrain economic growth; and (c) it is distributing the burden of adjustment in an unequal manner. Consider each proposition in turn.

First, the fiscal adjustment embodied in the budgets of the central government has relied on a surplus in the capital account to finance a deficit in the revenue account.[40] This is because the focus of adjustment is on the fiscal deficit rather than the revenue deficit of the government. The broad contours and dimensions of the fiscal adjustment on part of the central government are set out in Table 11 which compares the first half of the 1990s with the second half of the 1980s. It shows that the gross fiscal deficit of the central government contracted from 8.4 per cent of the GDP in 1990–91 to 5.9 per cent of GDP in 1991-92; it went down to 5.7 per cent of the GDP in 1992–93 but rose to 7.7 per cent of GDP in 1993–94 and is estimated at 6.7 per cent of GDP in 1994–95. The consequent reduction in government borrowing has exercised two important influences. For one, it has reduced borrowing from the central bank and there is a significant contraction in the monetized deficit as a proportion of GDP. For another, it has arrested the continous increase in internal public debt as a proportion of GDP. However, the burden of interest payments as a proportion of GDP has continued its rise partly

Table 11 *Fiscal adjustment by the central government (as a percentage of GDP at market prices)*

	1985-86 to 1989-90	1990-91	1991-92	1992-93	1993-94	1994-95
Gross fiscal deficit	8.2	8.4	5.9	5.7	7.7	6.7
Revenue deficit	2.6	3.5	2.6	2.6	4.2	3.8
Monetized deficit	2.3	2.8	0.9	0.6	0.1	0.2
Internal debt	50.7	53.2	51.7	51.0	53.0	53.2
Interest payments	3.2	4.0	4.3	4.4	4.8	5.0
Money supply (M3) (percentage growth per annum)	17.6	15.1	18.5	15.7	18.2	21.2

Source : Reserve Bank of India, *Annual Report, 1993-94.*

Note : For 1994-95, the data on central government deficits are based on revised estimates presented in the *Union Budget 1995-96,* while the data on internal debt and interest payments are based on budget estimates reported in *Economic Survey, 1994-95.*

because of the earlier debt and partly because of the significantly higher interest rates on government securities.[41] But the real problem is that the revenue deficit of the central government at 2.6 per cent of the GDP in both 1991–92 and 1992–93 was the same as it was in the second half of the 1980s. It reached its highest level at 4.2 per cent of GDP in 1993–94 and is estimated at 3.8 per cent of GDP in 1994–95. The government has therefore continued to borrow as much as 2.6 per cent of the GDP every year for a long time, and now more than 4 per cent of GDP, to finance its consumption expenditure. In an ideal world, there should be a revenue surplus large enough to finance capital expenditure on defence and in the social sectors, where there are no tangible returns, so that borrowing is used only to finance expenditure that yields a future income flow to the exchequer. The reality in India, despite fiscal adjustment, is the opposite. Such a fiscal regime, which borrows to support consumption, is simply not sustainable in the medium term for it is bound to fuel inflationary pressures or strain the balance of payments, as in the recent past, and thus disrupt the process of growth.

Second, the process of fiscal adjustment has created a massive squeeze on public investment. This is borne out, at a macro-level, by the stagnation in gross capital formation at constant prices in the public sector as a whole, which is made up of the central government, the state governments and public enterprises.[42] This is attributable, in part, to the attempt at fiscal adjustment by the central government which has also reduced the degrees of freedom for state governments. And the impact on resources made available by the central government for public investment is indeed significant. In the Union Budgets for 1991–92, 1992–93 and 1993–94, the period of adjustment, the provision for capital expenditure in the central plan and in central plan assistance for the states — perhaps the best aggregate measure of resources allocated to finance public investment — remained almost unchanged in nominal terms at about the same level as in 1990–91.[43] It is obvious that these budget provisions did not even compensate for the inflation, let alone the substantial exchange rate depreciation which would have raised the rupee costs of aid-financed investment, so that public investment certainly declined in real terms.[44] The resource crunch was even more acute for public investment in infrastructure. Table 12 shows that the budget support for key infrastructure sectors — energy, transport and communications — registered a significant decline not only as a proportion of the total central government expenditure but also in nominal terms. It is worth noting that, between 1989–90 and 1993–94, such budget support for infrastructure contracted by 46 per cent in real terms and dropped from 1.75 per cent of GDP to 0.81 per cent of GDP. These cuts in the public investment, particularly those on infrastructure, are bound to constrain the supply response of the economy in the medium term. The problem may be accentuated because the evidence available in India, both from the past and from the present, suggests that public investment crowds-in rather than crowds-out private investment. Indeed, the period from 1991–92 to 1993–94 also experienced a stagnation in gross domestic capital formation in the private sector so that, at constant prices, the trend in private investment was the same as in public investment.[45] It would seem that the squeeze on public investment, combined with fiscal adjustment and monetary discipline, had a dampening effect on private investment. If there is no increase in the level of investment in real terms, economic growth is bound to be constrained.

Third, the distribution of the burden of adjustment so far has been unequal. This is apparent from the evidence presented in Table 12 on the trends in expenditure from the Union Budget on the social

Table 12 *Central government expenditure on infrastructure, social sectors and poverty programmes : 1989-90 to 1993-94.*

Expenditure on	1989-90	1990-91	1991-92	1992-93	1993-94
Infrastructure					
in rupees million	79360	71370	63480	67570	63390
as a percentage of total central government expenditure	8.54	6.78	5.70	5.51	4.47
as a percentage of GDP	1.75	1.34	1.04	0.96	0.81
at constant 1980-81 prices (Rs. million)	39010	31680	24870	24055	20887
Social Sectors					
in rupees million	47620	53800	58810	67390	79060
as a percentage of total central government expenditure	5.13	5.11	5.27	5.49	5.57
as a percentage of GDP	1.05	1.01	0.96	0.96	1.01
at constant 1980-81 prices (Rs. million)	23410	23880	23040	23990	26050
Poverty alleviation programes					
in rupees million	27690	26780	22820	31980	45210
as a percentage of total central government expenditure	2.98	2.54	2.05	2.61	3.19
as a percentage of GDP	0.61	0.50	0.37	0.45	0.57
at constant 1980-81 prices (Rs. million)	13610	11890	8940	11380	14897

Source : Government of India, *Union Budget* documents, Expenditure Budget 1993-94, 1994-95 and 1995-96, Volume 1 : for data on sectoral and total expenditure.

Notes : a. The expenditure includes both plan expenditure and non-plan expenditure.

b. Social sectors correspond to the budgetary classification of social services such as education, health, family welfare, water supply, sanitation, housing, urban development, welfare of backward classes, labour, labour welfare, social welfare and nutrition. Infrastructure includes energy, transport and communications. The budget allocation for rural development corresponds almost exactly with central government expenditure on poverty alleviation programmes.

c. The expenditure–GDP ratios are calculated as a percentage of GDP at current market prices (data on GDP are from CSO, *National Accounts Statistics).*

d. Expenditure at current prices has been converted into expenditure at constant 1980-81 prices by using the deflator for GDP at factor cost. The conversion factors are obtained from CSO, *National Accounts Statistics,* August, 1994 and *Quick Estimates of National Income,* February, 1995.

sectors and on poverty alleviation programmes. It is not sufficient to examine these trends in terms of nominal values because of inflation and as a proportion of the total central government expenditure because of expenditure cuts. Therefore, Table 12 also considers the trends in such expenditure at constant prices and as a proportion of the GDP. The allocations for the social sectors — education, health, family welfare, water supply, sanitation, housing, urban development, social welfare of the under-privileged, nutrition and labour welfare — registered an increase in nominal terms and in their share of total expenditure. However, this expenditure stagnated in real terms and remained unchanged as a proportion of the GDP. Budget support for poverty alleviation programmes declined in nominal terms and as a proportion of total expenditure in 1991–92 although it recovered somewhat in 1992–93 and rose in 1993–94. But, at constant prices or as a proportion of GDP, expenditure on poverty programmes in both 1991–92 and 1992–93 was lower than it was in 1989–90 and 1990–91 and was not discernibly higher in 1993–94. It need hardly be stressed that in a period of stabilization and adjustment, resources provided for social services and for the poor should be increased rather than decreased or just maintained in real terms.

I recognize that it is not entirely appropriate to consider central government expenditure on the social sectors and on poverty alleviation programmes in isolation, because a large proportion of the expenditure on social services and some part of the expenditure on poverty programmes is financed by the state governments. But if we wish to consider the impact of fiscal adjustment, a focus on central government expenditure is unavoidable. What is more, the above conclusion is borne out by the evidence available on performance indicators in terms of quantitative achievements in the two major poverty alleviation programmes for rural India. This is set out in

Table 13 *Performance indicators : Poverty alleviation programmes 1989–90 to 1993–94*

	1989-90	1990-91	1991-92	1992-93	1993-94
Integrated rural development programme : families assisted (million)	3.35	2.90	2.54	2.07	2.54
Jawahar Rozgar Yojana : employment generated (million man-days)	864.4	874.6	808.1	778.3	1023.7

Source : Ministry of Rural Development, *Annual Reports.*

Table 13. The number of families assisted under the Integrated Rural Development Programme, which seeks to promote self-employment among the rural poor by providing productive assets or inputs through a mix of subsidies and bank credit, declined steadily from 3.4 million in 1989–90 to 2 million in 1992–93 and, despite some recovery, remained at 2.5 million in 1993–94. The employment generated under the Jawahar Rozgar Yojana, which seeks to create employment for the rural poor on works that are meant to create productive assets in the rural sector, also declined from 864 million man-days in 1989–90 to 778 million man-days in 1992–93, but rose to 1024 million man-days in 1993–94. In both, the decline was pronounced during the 1991–92 and 1992–93, followed by a restoration in 1993–94. Clearly, the real value of resources made available for poverty alleviation programmes diminished for some time, and did not register the necessary increase thereafter, as a consequence of fiscal adjustment in the process of stabilization.

It is my belief that the fiscal adjustment should have come from a more appropriate mix of expenditure-cuts and revenue-raising instead of relying exclusively on the former. In a period when the government is imposing a substantial burden on the poor through expenditure adjustment, the equity principle demands that the rich in particular, and the non-poor in general, share in this burden through their contribution to direct taxes. For this, it is absolutely essential to broaden the base for direct taxes so that a larger number of people are brought into the tax net and to deepen the structure of direct taxation by increasing the average rates of tax. The adjustment so far and the tax reform on the anvil appear to be moving in the opposite direction. The underlying philosophy, it would seem, is to provide comfort to the rich even if it means hardship for the poor. It is important to stress that such patterns of adjustment are nothing new, for they have been reproduced time after time in developing countries which embarked on stabilization and adjustment. Experience from elsewhere suggests that the squeeze on supply responses and the burden on the poor persists in the medium term.

B. Macro-economic implications

Let me now consider some elements of the interdependence between stabilization in the short term and adjustment in the medium term at a macro-level. There are four problems that deserve mention, for they appear to have surfaced in India.

The first problem is that a reduction in the fiscal deficit of the government does not always translate into a corresponding reduction in the current account deficit on the balance of payments for reasons explained earlier. This problem is borne out by the recent Indian experience which emerges from a comparison of Table 5 and Table 11. The current account deficit dropped to 0.8 per cent of GDP in 1991–92 mostly because of the severe import compression, rose to 2.2 per cent of GDP in 1992–93 despite the much reduced fiscal deficit of the central government, and dropped again to a negligible 0.1 per cent of GDP in 1993–94 even though the fiscal deficit increased by almost 2 percentage points. It is possible that this mismatch is attributable to the distribution of the changes in absorption between traded and non-traded goods, or to fluctuations in the gap between savings and investment in the private sector. Even in terms of orthodoxy, however, for a given excess of savings over investment in the private sector, it is the overall deficit in the government sector that determines the current account deficit. It would seem that in an endeavour to reduce its own fiscal deficit to satisfy conditionality, the central government has pushed out its borrowing requirements to the state governments and the public sector. Thus, it is possible that the overall deficit in the government sector has remained unchanged. In these circumtances, a sustainable reduction in the current account deficit may be easier to attain through a reduction in the trade deficit rather than the fiscal deficit.

The second problem is that the deflation implicit in the macro-economic adjustment inevitably leads to a slow down in growth and sometimes leads to contraction in output which, in turn, squeezes government revenues. This is also borne out by the recent Indian experience where the revenue shortfalls, particularly in the sphere of indirect taxes, are closely related to the contraction or stagnation of output in the organized industrial sector. If tax reform narrows that base of taxation at the same time, the burden on expenditure adjustment is even greater. The consequence may be deeper cuts in public investment which would choke supply responses and continued reduction in social expenditure which would impose a further burden on the poor.

The third problem is that exchange rate adjustments, so often an integral part of stabilization programmes, lead to a susbtantial devaluation which has several macro-economic implications and consequences for the balance of payments and inflation. The rupee did indeed depreciate by 50 per cent in nominal terms, *vis-a-vis* the US dollar. In an economy where external debt is a significant proportion of GDP and where much of the external debt is held by the government, as is the case in India, a large devaluation imposes a fiscal burden because the domestic resources needed to service the same debt increase *pari passu*. Similarly, in an economy that relies on foreign aid inflows to finance a part of its current account deficit, a substantial exchange rate depreciation slows down the utilization of external assistance[46] and thus adds to the strain on the balance of payments. There is evidence of this in India.[47] In the short run, a substantial devaluation may have an inflationary impact on prices through cost-push and mark-ups and a contractionary effect on output if it leads to a deterioration in the terms of trade. It is clear that the acceleration in inflation during 1991–92, as also its persistence in 1992–93, was spurred in part by the exchange rate adjustments just as the deterioration in the terms of trade during this period was, *inter alia,* attributable to the devaluation.[48]

The fourth problem arises when capital inflows such as portfolio investment become an important source of financing the current account deficit in the balance of payments. The economy then needs a high interest rate and strong exchange rate regime to sustain such inflows in terms of both profitability and confidence. This erodes the competitiveness of exports over time and enlarges the trade deficit. It is important to recognize the macro-economic implications. Larger trade deficits and current account deficits require larger portfolio investment inflows which, beyond a point, undermine confidence and create adverse expectations even if the government keeps the exchange rate pegged. But when the stifling of exports does ultimately force an exchange rate depreciation, confidence may simply collapse and lead to capital flight. These problems have indeed surfaced in several Latin American economies. And the recent Mexican experience suggests that any stabilization of the balance of payments based on portfolio investment or similar capital flows is fragile. It is early days yet, but the conflicting pressures on the exchange rate are already discernible in India.

In considering the medium term, the discussion can not be complete without reference to the mode of adjustment at a macro-level and its implications for the transition from stabilization to growth in India. Table 14 sets out the evidence on saving and

Table 14 *Saving and investment rates in India (as a percentage of GDP/NDP at current market prices)*

	1989-90	1990-91	1991-92	1992-93	1993-94
Gross domestic saving	24.0	23.9	23.1	20.0	20.2
Net domestic saving	15.7	15.8	14.5	10.8	11.1
Gross domestic investment	26.7	27.4	24.2	22.0	20.4
Net domestic investment	18.7	19.5	15.6	13.0	11.4

Source : CSO, *National Accounts Statistics,* August, 1994 (for 1989-90 to 1991-92) and *Quick Estimates of National Income,* February, 1995 (for 1992-93 and 1993-94).

Note : The data for 1992-93 are provisional while the data for 1993-94 are quick estimates.

investment rates in the economy. The nature of macro-economic adjustment is apparent from the fact that as a proportion of GDP, both gross domestic saving and gross domestic investment have registered a sharp decline during the period of stabilization from 1991–92 to 1993–94. So much so that, between 1990–91 and 1993–94, the saving–GDP ratio dropped by almost 4 percentage points while the investment–GDP ratio dropped by 7 percentage points. The decline in net domestic saving and net domestic investment, as proportion of NDP, was even more pronounced. It would appear that the process of macro-economic adjustment is based on an investment squeeze and in so far as investment still exceeds saving at a macro-level, the corresponding excess of imports over exports is being financed by foreign capital inflows. This must have adverse implications for economic growth in the medium term. Macro-economic adjustment that is conducive to growth needs to raise the investment–GDP ratio — and not lower it — by raising the domestic saving–GDP ratio and the export–GDP ratio instead of allowing a compensatory increase in the import–GDP ratio supported by external borrowing.

7. An Evaluation of Structural Reforms

It is, perhaps, too early to assess the impact of structural reform, for the Indian experience began in mid-1991 and supply responses emerge with a time lag. We do not as yet have any concrete evidence to validate or refute the hypothesis that structural reform would impart efficiency and dynamism to the process of economic growth. But some of the problems associated with the speed and the sequence of policy reform, mentioned earlier, appear to have surfaced in India. It is worth attempting an evaluation, even if brief, of the structural policy changes in relation to the industrial sector, the trade regime, foreign investment, foreign technology, the public sector and the financial sector.

A. *Industrial deregulation*

Industrial policy reform has removed barriers to entry for new firms and limits on growth in the size of existing firms. Investment decisions are thus no longer dependent upon government approval or constrained by State intervention. Industrial licencing has been abolished for all industries, except those specified, irrespective of levels of investment and the exceptions are few.[49] The law regulating monopolies has been amended to remove the threshold limit of Rs. 1 billion on the assets of large business houses and to eliminate the need for prior approval from the government for capacity expansion, capacity creation, amalgamation, mergers or takeovers on the part of such companies.[50]

It needs to be said that the dismantling of the complex regime of controls, particularly in the sphere of investment decisions, was both necessary and desirable. However, the removal of barriers to entry cannot be sufficient for restructuring in the industrial sector. The problems associated with barriers to exit must also be resolved. And it does not follow that deregulation, by itself, would reduce the degree of monopoly and increase the degree of competition among firms. This is a common but invalid presumption. It is possible that deregulation may not assure competition and may, in fact, induce rent-seeking behaviour. Some recent developments in India suggest that acquisitions, mergers or takeovers by firms in the industrial sector have enabled the enlarged corporate entity to capture a preponderant market share. It is possible to cite several examples. There are some that are significant and worth noting : the acquisition of TOMCO by Hindustan Lever ; the takeover of Godrej and Boyce by Procter and Gamble ; the merger of Parle and Coca Cola ; and the tie-up between Malhotras and Gillette. In these cases, the dominant market share so attained in a particular product range would either eliminate established competition or pre-empt potential competition.[51] This would simply not be permissible under anti-trust laws in most countries. Given the importance of scale economies in manufacturing, concerns about the concentration of economic power should not become a constraint on corporate growth. But in such situations the market must be governed either by calibrating competition or by suitable anti-trust legislation. In India, the law on monopolies has been diluted to abolish limits on growth but not strengthened to regulate monopolistic, restrictive or unfair trade practices so that it is nothing more than a watch-dog without teeth.

B. Trade liberalization

The object of trade policy reform implemented so far in India has been to eliminate discretionary controls on international trade transactions, to reduce the nominal as also the effective protection available to domestic industry and to bring domestic prices closer to world prices. In conformity with these objectives, there has been a rapid dismantling of quantitative restrictions on imports and exports, a substantial reduction of tariffs on imports combined with an abolition of subsidies on exports and several adjustments in the exchange rate which have led to a sizeable depreciation of the rupee.[52] The presumption is that this process would shift resources from the non-traded goods sector to the traded goods sector and that exposure to international competition would be conducive to efficiency in domestic firms.

In the presence of structural rigidities, however, the economy may not have the capacity to switch resources, whether labour or capital, from one sector to another as smoothly as orthodoxy believes is possible. And serious problems may arise in the transition. The rapid liberalization of the import regime which has dismantled import licensing and slashed customs duties across-the-board, except in the sphere of consumer goods, may force a de-industrialization in some sectors particularly capital goods. The substantial reduction in tariffs on imports of capital goods has, of course, reduced nominal protection, even after we allow for the exchange rate adjustments. But that is not all. In the absence of a commensurate reduction in the customs duties (and excise duties) on imported (and importable) manufactured intermediates, it is plausible to suggest that effective protection for the capital goods sector may have come down much more. This may also be the case for other manufacturing activities. Strangely enough, imports have been liberalized without establishing a comprehensive system of anti-dumping laws for domestic firms to invoke and to use whenever necessary. Such a system needs not only a legal framework but also a responsive government. If the industrial sector cannot cope with the pace of import liberalization or the practice of dumping, it may enforce closures rather than efficiency at a micro-level and reduce output and employment at the macro-level.

C. *Foreign investment and foreign technology*

The process of economic reform is seeking to increase the degree of openness of the economy to integrate it as soon as possible with the world economy. The endeavour is therefore not confined to trade flows. It extends to capital flows and technology flows. Consequently, the policy regime for foreign investment and foreign technology has been liberalized at a rapid pace so that prior government approval is the exception and not the rule.[53] It would seem that the primary objective is to enlarge non-debt-creating capital flows, while technology acquisition and market access appear as secondary objectives. This perception is perhaps shaped by nagging concerns about the balance of payments. The liberal access to imports of technology is meant to facilitate technological upgradation and enhance international competitiveness in industry.

The approach adopted, however, does not recognize that policy regimes may be necesary but are not sufficient to stimulate inflows of direct foreign investment. The recent Indian experience suggests that direct investment by international firms is on the increase, but the actual inflows are modest as a proportion of total foreign capital inflows and marginal as a proportion of total investment in the economy. The sectoral composition of this investment, concentrated mostly in consumer goods destined for the home market, is not surprising given the unequal income distribution and the associated pattern of demand combined with the prohibitive protection and the associated profitability. In my judgement, the increase in direct foreign investment is likely to be modest rather than phenomenal and nowhere near enough to become an important source of financing either the current account deficit in the balance of payments or investment in the economy. It is for this reason perhaps that the government has extended the liberalization of the policy regime further to portfolio investment on generous terms for foreign institutional investors.[54] In effect, this implies convertibility on the capital account for portfolio investment, without any lock-in period, even before attaining meaningful convertibility on the current account. Given the speculation and manipulation that characterizes Indian capital markets, this may turn out to be an expensive method of obtaining foreign capital. It could also be a possible source of destablizing capital outflows. Experience suggests that, in the early stages, such liberalization is quite unnecessary and very often susceptible to capital flight.[55] It must also be recognized that such financial flows, which finance current account deficits for a time, may not be transformed into investment in real terms in a world where transactions in the secondary market are dominant.

Similarly, the approach adopted fails to recognize the fact that imports of technology cannot be a substitute for domestic technological capabilities. The liberalization of technology imports could lead to a multiplicity of imports by several firms at a point in time and a recurrence of imports by the same firm over a period of time. The discipline of the market would, of course, place some limits on this process but it is possible that domestic technological capabilities may be stifled. Yet, an economy which industrializes should be able to move from importation to absorption and adaptation of technology through diffusion to the stage of innovation, at least in some sectors, on the path to sustained industrialization. In other words, the acquisition of technology through imports must, after a time, be followed by the development of technological capabilities. This cannot happen simply with an open regime for the import of technology. It needs the guiding and supportive role of the State, with strategic intervention in calibrating the import regime, providing resources for R&D and evolving procurement policies. Such intervention has been a necessary condition for technological development among the latecomers to industrialization not only in Asia but also elsewhere.[56]

D. Restructuring the public sector

In the sphere of public sector reform, it would seem that the main objectives of the government are to reduce the activities of the public sector, to facilitate the closure of sick units in the public sector and to ease the burden on the exchequer on account of the public sector.[57] It has been emphasized that the public sector should focus only on those sectors which are strategic and high-technology or constitute an integral part of the essential infrastructure. It has been announced that public sector enterprises which are chronically sick would be referred to the Board of Industrial and Financial Reconstruction, which would decide whether these units can be effectively reconstituted or whether they should be closed down. The centre-piece of public sector reform, however, is disinvestment of government equity up to 20 per cent, subsequently extended to 49 per cent, in selected public sector enterprises in an endeavour to impart a commercial orientation to enterprises in the public sector.

In comparison with other spheres, reforms in the public sector have been shallow and superficial. The articulated objectives are limited and inappropriate while their pursuit is half-hearted. The number of industries reserved for the public sector stands reduced but there has been no systematic review of the portfolio of public investment that might lead to restructuring or rationalization. There are some steps in terms of legislative amendments and administrative arrangements that may make it possible to close units in the public sector and retrench workers with suitable compensation. Much of this, however, remains in the sphere of intentions, for the political constituencies for such changes have not yet been created. However, the aim of easing the burden imposed by the public sector on the exchequer is being pursued with vigour.

The dominant motive underlying the sale of government equity in the public sector is the desire to mobilize resources for the exchequer. This is borne out by reality.[58] The capital receipts from such asset sales, in the range of Rs.25 billion per annum, have been absorbed in the Union Budget to reduce the borrowing needs, hence the fiscal deficit, of the central government. In terms of macro-economic management, it would obviously be desirable to use capital receipts from such disinvestment to retire public debt or even to mop up excess liquidity as an anti-inflationary measure. From the perspective of the public sector, it would be preferable to use the proceeds from the sale of government equity, at least in part, to restructure public enterprises. It is also a matter of concern that the *modus operandi* for the sale of shares of public enterprises is neither transparent nor at arms-length. What is worse, many of these shares have been sold at prices that are significantly below their market value. At the same time, non-plan budget support to the public sector, used mainly to finance losses, has been progressively withdrawn and now almost eliminated, which has obviously reduced government expenditure but has done nothing to ease the difficulties of such firms. The underlying philosophy, it seems, is to meet the needs of the government in the short run rather than to resolve the problems of the public sector in the medium term even though the long-term interests of the government coincide with the latter.

This approach to public sector reform which emphasizes asset sales and closures represents the most rudimentary forms of privatization and restructuring. It is neither adjustment nor reform. It may imply selling the flagships and keeping the tramp-ships, or sending white elephants to the slaughter house, but there is no systematic attempt to address problems of efficiency and productivity. We also need to remember from experience elsewhere—for example Britain—that privatization is a good strategy to impose discipline on the public sector so long as it is a potential, credible threat. It loses its virtue as soon as it becomes a reality.

E. Financial deregulation and liberalization

The objective of financial sector reform is to improve the profitability of the state-owned commercial banking system and the functioning of the domestic capital market on the presumption that the discipline imposed by market forces would make both more efficient.[59] The reforms in the context of commercial banks seek to improve profitability and restore financial health. The actual and the intended reductions in the statutory liquidity ratio (the minimum percentage of deposits that banks must hold in government securities) and the cash reserve ratio are meant to ensure that resources made available in the form of bank deposits are not preempted by the government but released for the private sector. The complex structure of differential interest rates charged and paid by the commercial banks has been simplified and rationalized largely through deregulation. It is hoped that this would help reduce the squeeze on the profitability of commercial banks. In parallel, interest rates on long-period government securities have been raised closer to market levels. This is meant to reduce the burden on commercial banks that was implicit in preemptive government borrowing. The government has also introduced new guidelines for income recognition, asset classification, provisioning requirements and capital adequacy in the commercial banking system. These accounting practices and prudential norms are expected to conform to international standards within a specified time horizon. The reforms in the capital market seek to finance investment in the private sector and attract foreign portfolio capital. Interest rates in the domestic capital market have been deregulated and the need for prior government approval of the size and the price of equity issues in the primary capital market has been dispensed with. It is believed that the capital market would be disciplined by market forces while a newly constituted Securities and Exchange Board of India would establish rules and regulations to govern the stock market and its intermediaries.

Financial sector reforms, implemented so far in India, have sought to reduce interventions practiced by the government and controls exercised by the central bank. A restructuring of the financial sector was clearly necessary, but this approach is characterized by some important limitations. First, the deregulation of interests rates has several implications. For one, it would now be difficult to use interest rates as a means of influencing resource allocation in the private sector. This may turn out to be a mistake because the use of interest rates is a strategic method of guiding the allocation of scarce investible resources in a market economy. For another, interest rates on government securities have been raised significantly. This may or may not lead to the development of a secondary market for government securities which would make government debt marketable, but it would definitely increase the burden of public debt on the exchequer. In an economy where the domestic debt of the government is large as a proportion of GDP and interest payments already preempt a substantial proportion of government expenditure, the problems of macro-management may be accentuated. Second, the introduction of accounting practices and prudential norms in conformity with international standards is obviously desirable but would require large provisions for non-performing assets in the portfolio of commercial banks. This is bound to erode net worth and would necessitate a larger equity base. In the Union Budgets, the government has thus made a provision of Rs.57 billion in 1993–94 and Rs.56 billion in 1994–95 for such recapitalization in the form of new government bonds. In other words, the government would borrow, creating a substantial interest burden, to recapitalize banks so that they can, in effect, write off bad loans ; this constitutes as much of a loan-waiver as any other. Third, the assumption that market forces, supported by a newly constituted Securities and Exchange Board of India, would suffice to discipline the capital market is somewhat heroic in a situation where, at least so far, trading malpractices abound, disclosure rules are almost non-existent and investor protection is slender. There is a clear need to plan the transition with care. The above limitations suggest that the government has embarked on deregulation and liberalization in the financial sector without the necessary planning of its temporal sequence and without a careful consideration of its wider implications.

In sum, financial sector reform in India is based on the premise that the commercial banking system and the domestic capital market are over-regulated and under-governed. This presumption is broadly correct. However, the process of reform unfolded so far suggests that deregulation has dispensed with the over-regulation, but the system remains under-governed because institutional and legal frameworks that would govern the market have not yet been put in place. This mismatch or asymmetry is fraught with risk.

8. Economic Liberalization : The Wider Context

IT IS ESSENTIAL to situate the process of economic liberalization in India in its wider context and in a longer-term perspective. The reason is twofold. First, the debate on reforms tends to focus on what is said or done but a systematic assessment should also consider what is not said or not done. Second, the origin of reforms and the conjuncture in which these are introduced are important determinants of success or failure. The discussion that follows addresses these issues.

It is important to consider the sectoral components of structural reform but it is also necessary to consider the reform process as a whole. Such a perspective reveals two shortcomings in the Indian experience. Economic liberalization is about bringing market prices closer to efficiency prices and allowing individuals, households or firms more freedom to make economic decisions. This means a reduced role for the State. But co-ordinating the market through rules that govern may in turn imply a need for more State intervention somewhere and different forms of State intervention elsewhere in the pursuit of development objectives. There is no thinking, let alone clarity, about this redefined role of the State. This is the first shortcoming. The restructuring of economies, if it is to be a success, must not only introduce correctives to eliminate weaknesses but also plan consolidation to build on strengths that emerge from the past development experience. It would seem that the reform process in India, based on a standardized blueprint from elsewhere, does not incorporate such learning from the past. This is the second shortcoming. Consider each in turn.

The belief that markets know best is associated with an unstated presumption that State intervention is not needed or is counter-productive in the process of industrialization. This is ahistorical. Experience from the second half of the twentieth century suggests that the guiding and the supportive role of the State has been at the foundation of successful development among late industrializers. Even among the East Asian countries, which are often cited as success stories that depict the magic of the market place, the visible hand of the State is much more in evidence than the invisible hand of the market.[60] In the earlier stages of industrialization, State intervention creates the conditions for the development of industrial capitalism by establising a physical infrastructure through government investment, developing human resources through education or facilitating institutional change through agrarian reform. In the later stages of industrialization, State intervention is functional or strategic rather than conducive but remains crucial.

Functional State intervention may seek to correct for market failures, both general and specific, or it may seek to estabish rules that govern markets. Strategic State intervention, interlinked across activities or sectors, may seek to attain broader, long term objectives of development. It is possible to cite several examples. Exchange rate policy is not simply a tactical matter of getting-prices-right but may turn out to be a strategic matter if deliberately undervalued exchange rates, maintained over a period of time, provide an entry into the world market for differentiated manufactured goods. The structure of interest rates is not just about allowing market forces to determine the price of capital, but may be a strategic method of guiding the allocation of scarce investible resources. Restrictions on the use of foreign brand names is not so much an inward-looking attitude if it is perceived as a strategic means of buying time to develop national brand names that become acceptable in world markets after a lag. In this manner, State intervention may constitute an integral part of any strategy of industrialization that endeavours to strengthen capabilities and develop institutions rather than rely on incentives or markets alone.[61] This is the most important lesson that emerges from the East Asian experience. Strategic intervention by the State, not only in the realm of industrial policy and technology policy but also in the sphere of trade policy, rather than a reliance on market forces alone, is a vital factor underlying efficiency and dynamism in industrialization and growth.[62]

There is, of course, government failure just as much as market failure, for neither governments nor markets are, or can be, perfect.[63] In theory, it may be possible to remedy market failure by State intervention. In practice, governments may lack the ability or the willingness to intervene efficiently. The wrong kind of State intervention can induce rent-seeking unproductive activities, but so can unregulated markets. The right kind of State intervention can channel rents created in the process of industrialization, through market forces, into productive uses. It is the nature and the form of State intervention that matters. The experience of excessive State intervention associated with government failures, however, should not lead to the conclusion that minimal State intervention is the best or that market failures do not matter. We appear to have moved from a widespread belief, prevalent in the 1950s, that the State could do nothing wrong to a gathering conviction, fashionable in the 1990s, that the State can do nothing right. These are caricature perceptions. The reality is more complex than simplified paradigms that may be in or out of fashion. In a world of uneven development, characterized by rapid technical progress, ever-changing comparative advantage and imperfect market structures, the role of governments in the industrialization process remains vital and could account for the difference between success and failure. For industrialization is not only about getting-prices-right ; industrialization is also about getting-state-intervention-right.

In India, as in Eastern Europe, perceptions have been so strongly influenced by the counter-productive role of State intervention in the past that we have not yet recognized the possibilities of a creative interaction between the State and the market. Hence there is no attempt at rethinking and redefining the role of the State. This India syndrome of rejection rather than correction has other dimensions which may also have serious implications. The perception of the reformers, stated in over-simplified form, is that the strategy of the past four decades was a complete mistake and that salvation lies in the new *mantras* : get prices right, rely on markets and integrate with the world economy. Consequently, the reform process in India stresses the need to eliminate weaknesses or what went wrong but neglects the possibilities of building on strengths or what turned out right. This provides a sharp contrast with the experience of China where the transition from central planning to market socialism, managed with success, corrected for the weaknesses but built on the strengths of the Mao era. But that is not all. There is a striking asymmetry in our learning, for we have chosen to ignore two basic failures.

In a long-term perspective, among the most important failures to emerge from the Indian development experience, I have argued earlier, are the neglect of human resources and the neglect of agrarian reform. The present agenda for reform simply does not address these failures because there is so little concern about development objectives in the long term. It is worth noting that there is no mention of education in the reform process let alone human resource development. Unless we invest enough in human beings, productivity increase may not follow structural reform. And in the absence of a sufficiently developed human infrastructure, the benefits of integrating with the world economy may simply elude us. It is also striking that the entire discourse about structural reform proceeds as if the agricultural sector does not exist or, if it exists, it does not matter. This is indeed puzzling in an economy where the agricultural sector contributes one-third of the GDP and employs more than two-thirds of the work-force. And it is not as if the agricultural sector is without its structural rigidities or structural imbalances. What is more, the process of stabilization, adjustment and reform may have a profound impact on the output and prices in the agricultural sector.[64] It may accentuate inequalities in the distribution of output and incomes between regions which would have political implications. It may increase domestic prices of wage goods produced in the agricultural sector and erode food security which would have social consequences. Yet, we discuss economic liberalization in an economy with a large rural hinterland as if the agricultural sector is irrelevant.

In this context, it is important to emphasize that institutional reform in the agricultural sector, the spread of education in society and, above all, the strategic role of State intervention have been, in a sense, necessary conditions for capitalist development among late industrializers, particularly the success stories in East Asia that are now perceived as role models. It would seem that the architects of economic liberalization in India do not recognize the significance of these lessons which emerge from experience elesewhere. Yet, there is a naive presumption that a reliance on the market is both necessary and sufficient to emulate the East Asian economies. There is no recognition that while lessons are important, it is simply not possible to replicate development experience because economies are characterized by specificities in time and space. The implications of the origins and the conjuncture are altogether ignored.

The process of economic reform is either strategy-based or crisis-driven. There are relatively few examples of strategy-based-reform except for the success stories among the East Asian countries. Crisis-driven-reform is much more common : a crisis in the economy mostly on account of external debt provided the impetus in Latin America, sub-Saharan Africa and South Asia, while a collapse of the political system gave the push in Eastern Europe. The probability of success or failure is strongly influenced by the economic or political origins of the reform process.

Economic reform that represents a natural transition in the strategy of development is based in social formations and is shaped by political processes that provide the constituencies. Such a reform process can both sustain and succeed in part because it creates a capacity to manage problems of transition. For one, the change is acceptable to polity and society. For another, the speed and the sequence of adjustment can be absorbed by the economy.

Economic reform which is crisis-driven, irrespective of whether the crisis is an external shock or an internal convulsion, is more difficult to sustain and less likely to succeed. The reasons are manifold and complex. Some have been considered earlier while discussing problems of transition. But there are others which deserve to be highlighted. First, the preoccupation with stabilization in the short term and adjustment or reform in the medium term, which is natural for multilateral financial institutions, leads to confusion between tactics and strategies or means and ends in the minds of governments. This often leads to a neglect of the long term in terms of development objectives, particularly those that cannot be defined in terms of performance criteria in the sphere of economics or tangible gains in the realm of politics. Second, during such transitions, for the majority of the people, the costs of the reform process surface soon while the benefits are a distant promise. In the absence of supportive constituencies, if reform is not absorbed by the economy or not acceptable to the polity, disillusionment sets in and even the necessary and desirable components of reform are discredited. Third, the political and social coalitions which support or oppose reforms determine whether the process will ultimately be sustainable. If the support comes from the rich, the literati and the influential who are vocal and capture most of the benefits, while the opposition comes from the poor and the unorganized who are silent and bear most of the costs, economic liberalization accentuates social divisions and political alienation. The coalitions for and against may, of course, be more complex in their composition but it is the distribution of the benefits and the costs, together with their respective size in terms of population, that would determine their strengths and shape outcomes. These problems are obviously more acute in democratic regimes but are not altogether absent in authoritarian regimes.

9. Some Conclusions

IT MAY BE somewhat premature to draw definite lessons from the experience of economic liberalization in India. But it is possible to draw some conclusions that emerge from this essay. In doing so, it would be my endeavour to sketch the contours of an alternative view. The discussion which follows attempts to set out the framework for an alternative, in terms of what is to be done, at an analytical level. I would like to stress, however, that my reflections can only provide a modest beginning in the identification of correctives and strategies for the future.

The restructuring of an economy over time has three dimensions : the management of demand, the management of incentives and the development of capabilities and institutions. The object of managing the demand is to influence the level and the composition of demand—hence output and employment—in the economy, mostly in the short term. The object of designing incentives is to induce supply responses and coax productivity increases, mostly in the medium term. The object of building capabilities at a micro-level and institutions at a meso-level is to create a milieu that imparts efficiency and dynamism to the growth process, mostly in the long term.

Each of these dimensions of restructuring has a close correspondence with the respective time horizons. But it is not possible to separate demand, supply and capabilities or institutions in this manner because there is an interdependence and an interaction which leads to spill-overs. It would take too long to set up a complete matrix. Some examples would suffice. For instance, aggregate demand management in the short term, which is part of a stabilization programme, may squeeze supply responses in the medium term. Similarly, incentive management, say in the form of import liberalization, may impact on the level of demand in the short term at a macro-level if it switches expenditure away from home-produced goods and may affect capabilities in the long term if it enforces closures rather than efficiency at a micro-level. Or, State intervention meant to support the development of capabilities and institutions in the long term, say strategic industrial policy, may affect incentive structures in the medium term and agregate demand in the short term.

In my judgement, economic liberalization in India, which is attempting to restructure the economy, is overwhelmingly concerned with the management of incentives and the supply side in a medium-term perspective. Some attention is paid to the management of demand in the short term but this is limited to the quest for stabilization. There is no recognition that the development of capabilities and institutions has a long-term significance. This approach, evolved by the Bretton Woods institutions—which has been adopted in India and elsewhere—cannot make for success. The restructuring of incentives in isolation often has an adverse effect on demand in the short term and capabilities in the long term. The better alternative, which considers all three dimensions, should recognize possible contradictions so as to avoid them and should recognize potential complementarities so as to exploit them.

The management of demand, mostly internal but also external, is based on fiscal policy and monetary policy combined with exchange rate policy. In India, it has been concerned with stabilization.[65] But the mix of stabilization policies has been inappropriate. Aggregate demand management through fiscal adjustment and monetary policy should have squeezed imports and consumption of the non-poor, instead of investment and consumption of the poor. In a situation where incomes are low, consumption levels of the poor need to be protected by restraining inflation and maintaining public expenditure destined for the poor. The mode of adjustment on the demand side, I believe, is crucial for it can either stimulate or stifle growth. Therefore, fiscal adjustment should not rely excessively on expenditure reduction but should also attempt to increase income of the government. At the same time, it is essential to raise the level and the rate of investment in the economy. For this, it is necessary to increase public investment, particularly in infrastructure where private investment (whether domestic or foreign) is not forthcoming. As far as possible, such public investment should be financed out of higher tax and non-tax revenues. To some extent, borrowing can also be used for this purpose, provided that investments financed by borrowed resources yield adequate returns. The size of the fiscal deficit is less important than the use or the cost of borrowing. It is the revenue deficit which requires borrowing to finance consumption expenditure of the government that must be progressively reduced and rapidly eliminated. The fetishism about reducing the fiscal deficit despite a burgeoning revenue deficit, or eliminating the monetized deficit despite the much higher cost of borrowing, is entirely misplaced. It is time to give up cosmetic devices which conceal the problem or postpone the day of reckoning and seek a sustainable solution to the fiscal crisis. Similarly, the balance of payments adjustment should be based on an expansion in exports rather than a stagnation in imports. The reliance on unsustainable and unstable capital inflows to finance current account deficits is a mistake. Direct foreign investment which provides non-debt-creating and investment-financing capital inflows is preferable as a source of external finance. But it has implications for domestic capabilities in the long term which must be recognized.

The management of incentives, motivated by the object of minimizing costs and maximizing efficiency at a micro-level, is based on a set of policies that are intended to increase competition between firms in the market place. Domestic competition is sought to be provided through deregulation in investment decisions, in the financial sector and in labour markets. Foreign competition is sought to be provided through openness in trade, investment, capital and technology flows. There are the obvious correctives. For one, the speed of change must be calibrated so that it can be absorbed by the economy. For another, the sequence of change must be planned with reference to an order of priorities. In both, whether speed or sequence, deregulation and openness must be consistent with the other dimensions of restructuring in the short term and in the long term. There are, however, problems beyond simple correctives which must be addressed and resolved. First, it is essential to establish rules that govern markets, for the market is a good servant but a bad master whether in the sphere of industrial deregulation, trade liberalization or financial sector reform. Second, a focus on sectoral components of reform may lead to a situation where the structure of incentives as a whole is inappropriate. For instance, the present mix of tax reform and financial liberalization rewards finance capital more than industrial capital. But industrial capitalism is made on shop floors and not in stock markets. It is important to avoid the dangers of what Keynes described as casino capitalism. Third, it must be recognized that incentives may be necessary but are not sufficient and that there is nothing automatic about competition. Policy regimes can allow things to happen but cannot cause things to happen. The creation of competitive markets that enforce efficiency may, in fact, require strategic intervention through industrial policy, trade policy or financial policy.

The development of capabilities and institutions is an essential foundation for international competitiveness. This is clearly established by the experience of the successful latecomers to industrialization, particularly in Asia but also elsewhere. It would seem that the third dimension of restructuring has been neglected altogether in India's economic liberalization even by those who wish to capture the benefits from integration with the world economy or dream of becoming global players. This must be corrected so that the long term objectives of development receive the much-deserved attention. In this context, there are three points that I would emphasize. First, the importance of education in particular and human resource development in general cannot be stressed enough. It is vital. Second, the acquisition of technological and managerial capabilities is absolutely essential. It must be ensured that the structure of incentives helps in building and does not end up stifling, these capabilities. Third, the creation of institutions that would regulate, streamline and facilitate the functioning of markets is clearly necessary. This will require planning and take time. In each of these pursuits, strategic forms of State intervention are of the essence. Therefore, the government simply cannot afford to abdicate its role in the belief that markets know best. It is only a creative interaction between the State and the market, which evolves in a dialectical manner with the passage of time, that can foster the development of capabilities and institutions in the process of industrialization.

In conclusion, let me return to some simple macro-economics and the wider context of politics. It is obvious that an acceleration in the rate of growth of the economy is essential. Such growth can come, in part, from an increase in the productivity of investment through an appropriate restructuring of the economy. But only in part. Ultimately, sustained economic growth also requires an increase in the investment–GDP ratio. The strategy, then, should be to sustain higher investment rates by raising the export–GDP ratio and the domestic savings–GDP ratio and not by allowing a compensatory increase in the import–GDP ratio supported by foreign capital inflows. This underlines the significance of increasing exports and raising domestic savings. The former is recognized. The latter, it appears, is forgotten. We also need to remember that economic growth is a necessary but not a sufficient condition for an improvement in the living conditions of the people. The process of growth must create employment and incomes for the poor. There is no other way to eradicate poverty.

It is obviously not possible to restructure an economy in the abstract without reference to the reality in the national context and the conjuncture in the international context. The restructuring of the economy in India, in terms of a better alternative based on the analytical framework set out above, must then also relate to the political framework of democracy at home and the changed force of circumstances in the world outside. The challenges must be met and the opportunities must be exploited by recognizing, and not by ignoring, political realities. In the national context, there are contradictions as also conflicts in economy, polity and society. Yet, there exists some degree of overlap between what is desirable in economics, feasible in politics and acceptable in society. In the international context, globalization of the world economy combined with a polarization of world politics has reduced the degrees of freedom for the nation state. But there remains some space for the pursuit of national economic interests. In both spheres, I believe, it is possible to match sensible economics with feasible politics.

Notes

1 The simple national income accounting identity $Y = C + I + X - M$ can be rewritten as $I - S = M - X$ given that $Y - C = S$. Let Ip and Sp denote investment and saving in the private sector. Let Ig, Sg, Cg, Eg and Yg denote investment, saving, consumption, expenditure and income respectively in the government sector.

$$\begin{aligned}
\text{Then, } I - S &= (Ip + Ig) - (Sp + Sg) \\
&= (Ip - Sp) + (Ig - Sg) \\
\text{In turn, } (Ig - Sg) &= [Ig - (Yg - Cg)] \\
&= [(Ig + Cg) - Yg] \\
&= (Eg - Yg) \\
\text{Therefore, } (M - X) &= (Ip - Sp) + (Eg - Yg)
\end{aligned}$$

2 For evidence on—and discussion of—the increase in the import intensity of domestic production during the 1980s, see Nayyar (1994 a). There was a similar increase in the import intensity of exports (Nayyar, 1988). It is worth noting that these developments were also recognized by the Economic Advisory Council to the Prime Minister (then chaired by Professor Sukhamoy Chakravarty), in its *Report on the Current Economic Situation and Priority Areas for Action*, Government of India, New Delhi, December 1989, pp.11–12.

3 It is worth noting that the evidence presented in Table 2 underestimates the size of, and the increase in, India's external debt during the 1980s as it does not include defence debt and short-term debt. Unfortunately, there is no published information on these two components of external debt for most of this period. Indeed, the official statistics on external debt are even more limited in their coverage.

4 The level of foreign exchange reserves was $ 1.2 billion in mid-January 1991 and $ 1.1 billion in end-June 1991 ; see Reserve Bank of India, *Bulletin*, monthly issues.

5 The data on the magnitude of short-term debt were published for the first time in the *Report of Policy Group and Task Force on External Debt Statistics of India*, Reserve Bank of India, Bombay, 1992.

6 The factors underlying this capital flight from non-resident deposits and its macro-economic implications are discussed, at some length, in Nayyar (1994 b).

7 The monetized deficit averaged 2.2 per cent of GDP during the period 1980–81 to 1984–85 and 2.3 per cent of GDP during the period 1985–86 to 1989–90. The average annual growth in broad money, M3, was 16.7 per cent and 17.6 per cent respectively in the same periods. see *Economic Survey 1990–91*, Ministry of Finance, Government of India, New Delhi, p.100, 124.

8 The share of direct taxes in the total revenues of the central government dropped from about 25 per cent in the late 1970s to less than 20 per cent in the late 1980s,

so that the share of indirect taxes rose from about 75 per cent to more than 80 per cent. Revenues from direct taxes collected by the central government were the equivalent of around 2.5 per cent of GDP in the late 1970s and 2.1 per cent of GDP in the late 1980s. On the other hand, revenues from indirect taxes collected by the central government were the equivalent of around 7 per cent of GDP in the late 1970s and 9 per cent of GDP in the late 1980s ; see *Indian Public Finance Statistics,* 1992, Ministry of Finance, Government of India, New Delhi, pp. 28-31.

9 The total expenditure of the central government increased from 16 per cent of GDP in 1980–81 to 20 per cent of GDP in 1985–86 and stayed above that level through the second half of the 1980s (these proportions have been calculated from data on expenditure in the *Economic and Functional Classification of the Central Government Budget* and *National Accounts Statistics,* annual issues).

10 The revenue surplus or the revenue deficit measures the difference between the revenue receipts of the government (made up of tax revenues plus non-tax revenues) and the non-investment expenditure of the government. The data for the 1970s are reported in *Indian Public Finance Statistics, 1992,* Ministry of Finance, Government of India, New Delhi, pp. 34–35 ; for data on the 1980s, *see* Table 1.

11 There is an extensive literature on this subject which considers the impact of foreign capital inflows on domestic savings in terms of both theory and evidence. *See,* for example, Griffin (1970) and Weisskopf (1972).

12 Bhagwati and Desai (1970), followed by Bhagwati and Srinivasan (1975), were among the first to provide an elaborate critique of industrialization India from a neo-classical perspective, suggesting that the policy framework led to economic inefficiency and resource misallocation while the cumulative effect of these policies became an obstacle to growth.

13 The exchange rate adjustments in July 1991 led to a depreciation of the rupee *vis-a-vis* the US dollar by 23.3 per cent and *vis-a-vis* the SDR by 21.7 per cent. There was a further depreciation of the rupee implicit in the introduction of a dual exchange rate system in March 1992 and the subsequent unification of the exchange rate in March 1993. Consequently, between end-June 1991 and end-June 1993, in nominal terms, the rupee depreciated by 50 per cent *vis-a-vis* the US dollar and 59 per cent *vis-a-vis* the SDR (calculated from data on exchange rates published by the Reserve Bank of India in its *Annual Reports*). The gross fiscal deficit of the central government was reduced from 8.4 per cent of GDP in 1990–91 to 5.9 per cent of GDP in 1991–92 and 5.7 per cent of GDP in 1992–93 (Table 11). There was a significant tightening of the monetary policy in 1991–92 as part of which the minimum interest rate on lending by commercial banks was raised to 18.5 per cent per annum ; but this has been lowered in stages since then (for details, *see* Reserve Bank of India, *Annual Reports*).

14 For an elaborate and systematic critique, *see* Taylor (1988).

15 The policy reform is described, at some length, in the *Economic Survey* published by the Ministry of Finance and the *Report on Currency and Finance* published by the Reserve Bank of India. For details of the initial changes, *see* also Government of India (1991a and 1991b). For an overview, and for an account of the subsequent changes, see Government of India (1993).

16 For a discussion of these earlier episodes of liberalization and the factors underlying the shift in emphasis in the strategy of industrialization, *see* Nayyar (1994a).

17 The rationale for the economic reforms introduced over the past three years and the necessity of departures from the earlier strategy of development is set out, at some length, by Bhagwati and Srinivasan (1993).

18 For a discussion of alternative hypotheses about inflation, *see* Taylor (1988).

19 See Cooper (1992), pp. 49–57.

20 For an analysis of the possible contractionary effects of a devaluation, *see* Krugman and Taylor (1978).

21 This did happen in Latin America where the 1980s are, in retrospect, described as the lost decade. Many countries in Eastern Europe, in their process of transition from planned systems to market economies, are experiencing similar difficulties.

22 There is an extensive literature on this subject. *See*, for example, Williamson (1983), Killick (1984), Taylor (1988), Williamson (1990) and Taylor (1993).

23 In the policy–based lending programmes of multilateral financial institutions, conditionalities begin with the classical areas of economic policy, but then extend to social institutions such as civil service systems or legal frameworks and political areas such as governance, human rights and democracy. In an evaluation of policy–based assistance to developing countries led by the adjustment based lending of the World Bank, Yenal observes : 'Designing economic and social policies—an avocation which can also be called policy engineering—provides immense satisfaction for all those interested in economics and politics... Soon the policy engineer finds himself attempting to do nothing short of what political leaders are supposed to do. This, of course, is a grave mistake...this can open the door to what some have called neo-colonialism and the imposition of external governance on what has to be national policies.' *See* O. Yenal, 'Development : A Critical Look at the Consensus', *The Economic Times*, New Delhi, 30 January 1992. The author, at the time that it was written, was the resident representative of the World Bank in India.

24 For evidence on the impact of structural adjustment on the social sectors, nutrition, health and living standards in developing countries, *see* Cornia, Jolly and Stewart (1987).

25 Some part of the monetary expansion, particularly during 1993–94, may have been attributable to the substantial accumulation of foreign exchange reserves.

26 The modest harvest in 1991–92 probably accentuated, while the bumper harvest in 1992–93 probably eased inflationary pressures and expectations in the economy.

27 *See* Table 9. For details of the changes in procurement prices and in issue prices for the public distribution system, *see Economic Survey, 1993–94*, pp. 67–68.

28 The amnesties, which were announced in the Union Budget for 1991–92, meant that no questions were asked about the sources of funds either for the bonds or for the remittances. It is reasonable to presume that most of the inflow facilitated a laundering of money which attained a legal status, whether it was held abroad in the form of bonds or returned home in the form of remittances.

29 The scheme of Foreign Currency (Banks and Others) Deposits was introduced in November, 1990 and abolished in July, 1992. The Non-Resident (non-repatriable) Rupee Deposit Scheme was introduced in late 1992, where the principal is non-repatriable but the interest is repatriable and the interest rates are significantly higher than in international capital markets. The Foreign Currency Non-Resident (Banks) Accounts Scheme was introduced in May, 1993. Under this scheme, the depositor is protected from the exchange rate risk but the risk is borne by the commercial bank accepting the deposit, unlike the earlier FCNR accounts where the exchange rate risk was met by the Reserve Bank of India. An exchange rate depreciation could then impose significant losses on commercial banks so that their willingness and ability to accept such deposits would depend upon a confidence that the exchange rate would be stable.

30 The evidence cited in this paragraph is obtained from the Reserve Bank of India, *Annual Report, 1993-94,* p.97 and pp.238–239.

31 In end-January, 1995, the level of foreign exchange reserves was $ 19.6 billion. The par value of the outstanding portfolio investment in end-December, 1994, was $ 6.5 billion. At the end of September, 1994, short-term debt with a maturity of one year or less was $ 2.8 billion, while the outstanding stock of repatriable deposits was $ 13.4 billion. For details, *see Economic Survey, 1994–95.*

32 This plausible hypothesis is confirmed by available evidence. The rate of growth of employment in the organized sector of the economy, including both the public sector and the private sector, dropped from 1.71 per cent in 1989–90 and 1.44 per cent in 1990–91 to 1.21 per cent in 1991–92 and 0.60 per cent in 1992–93 (*see* Ministry of Labour, *Annual Reports, 1993–94* and *1994–95*).

33 *See* Papola (1993). The labour force has grown at an average rate of 2.36 per cent per annum over the period from 1951 to 1992. Except for the 1960s, the average rate of growth of employment has been significantly lower throughout this period.

34 The employment elasticity for the economy as a whole declined from 0.61 during the period 1972–73 to 1977–78 to 0.55 during the period 1977–78 to 1983 and 0.38 during the period 1983 to 1987–88. The corresponding figures were 0.66, 0.49 and 0.36 respectively for the agricultural sector and 0.55, 0.42 and 0.26 respectively for the manufacturing sector. For details, *see* Planning Commission (1990).

35 For details on the evidence, methodology and estimates, *see* Planning Commission (1993).

36 For a detailed discussion on the implications and consequences of trade liberalization for the agricultural sector in India and its possible impact on domestic food prices, *see* Nayyar and Sen (1994).

37 For supporting evidence, *see Economic Survey,* 1993–94, pp.66–67 and *Economic Survey, 1994–95,* pp. 78–82. It is worth noting that retail prices in the public distribution system were significantly higher than the central issue prices : in some states the margin was as much as 20 per cent.

38 These percentages have been calculated, on a point-to-point basis, from the wholesale price index numbers for each of these commodity groups.

39 The available evidence on the trends at constant 1980-81 prices is as follows :

Year	NNP at factor cost per capita	Private final consumer expenditure per capita
1989–90	2160	1822
1990–91	2213	1855
1991–92	2167	1851
1992–93	2226	1839
1993–94	2282	1879

Source : *CSO, National Accounts Statistics.*

40 The distinction between the capital account and the revenue account is most simply stated as follows : transactions which affect the net wealth or debt position of the central government enter into the capital account, while transactions which affect the income or expenditure of the central government enter into the revenue account.

41 The change in the pattern of government borrowing may introduce an altogether new dimension to the problem of public debt. The resort to zero-coupon bonds on a significant scale, which began in 1993–94, may postpone both amortization and interest payments for some time, but could seriously accentuate difficulties for the exchequer when the bullet repayment is to be made.

42 In the public sector, gross domestic capital formation at 1980–81 prices was Rs.2,18,960 million in 1990–91, Rs.2,03,490 million in 1991–92, Rs.2,04,490 million in 1992–93 and Rs.2,04,400 million in 1993–94 (see *CSO National Accounts Statistics,* August 1994, p.53 and *Quick Estimates of National Income,* February, 1995, p.18). In real terms, therefore, public investment during the period of stabilization did not even recover to the level attained in 1990–91.

43 Capital expenditure in the central plan and in the central plan assistance to states and union territories was Rs.1,59,360 million in 1990–91, Rs.1,60,980 million in 1991–92, Rs.1,64,550 million in 1992–93 and Rs.1,70,660 million in 1993–94 (*see* Union Budget documents for respective years). The budget estimate for this provision in 1994–95 was Rs.1,85,200 million.

44 It is possible to assess the implications for the level of public investment in real terms if these budget provisions for capital expenditure in the central plan and in the central plan assistance to states and union territories are converted into constant prices using the GDP deflator. This calculation suggests that, at 1980-81 prices, such budget support declined from Rs.70,788 million in 1990–91 to Rs.62,348 million in 1991–92, Rs.58,580 million in 1992–93 and further to Rs.56,232 million in 1993–94.

45 In the private sector, gross domestic capital formation at 1980–81 prices was Rs.3,55,720 million in 1990–91, Rs.2,90,230 million in 1991–92, Rs.3,45,260 million in 1992–93 and Rs.3,09,740 million in 1993–94 (see *CSO National Accounts Statistics,* August, 1994, p.53 and *Quick Estimates of National Income,* February, 1995, p.18). There was, however, a redistribution within the private sector as investment in the private corporate sector rose while that in the household sector fell.

46 This happens for two reasons. First, in so far as aid finances the local-rupee-costs of investment or consumption, the foreign exchange equivalent of aid utilized drops *pari passu*. Second, in so far as aid finances the foreign-exchange-costs of investment projects, the matching or complementing contribution from the central government or the state governments to meet the rupee expenditure is not forthcoming because of the resource crunch or fiscal austerity, as a result of which aid utilization slows down.

47 In spite of the serious balance of payments problem, which required extraordinary capital flows to meet the financing need, the gross utilization of the external assistance (mostly project aid from bilateral or multilateral sources) registered a significant decline from $ 4,689 million during 1991–92 to $ 3,589 million during 1992–93 and $ 3,769 million during 1993–94 (see *Economic Survey,* 1994–95).

48 In 1991–92, the volume of exports rose by 7.5 per cent and the dollar value of exports fell by 1.5 per cent. In 1992–93, the volume of exports rose by 6.9 per cent while the dollar value of exports increased by 3.8 per cent (see *Economic Survey,* 1993–94).

49 For details, *see* Government of India (1991a). The exceptions are specified industries either reserved for the public sector (Annex I, p.10) or industries subject to compulsory licencing (Annex II, p.11) because of security concerns, environmental or safety factors and social concerns such as the desire to limit elitist consumption. Subsequent relaxations in April, 1993, have opened up much of the mining sector for private investment and industrial delicencing has been extended to consumer durables.

50 Ibid, p.6 and p.9.

51 There are similar examples of some mergers, acquisitions and takeovers by domestic firms, but the limited experience so far suggests that such a strategic response to deregulation has been more characteristic of large international firms.

52 Quantitative restrictions on most imports and exports except for specified negative lists have been abolished. (For details, *see* Government of India (1991b) and *Export–Import Policy : April 1992–March 1997,* Government of India, Ministry of Commerce, New Delhi, 31 March, 1992). Cash subsidies on exports were abolished in July, 1991. There has also been a substantial reduction in tariffs on imports over the past four years in the Union Budgets. The maximum duty rate was reduced to 150 per cent in the union budget for 1991–92, 110 per cent in 1992–93, 85 per cent in 1993–94, 65 per cent in 1994–95 and 50 per cent in 1995–96. The customs duties on imports of most capital goods were reduced to 80 per cent in July, 1991, 55 per cent in February, 1992, 35 per cent in February, 1993 and 25 per cent in February, 1994. A uniform rate of 25 per cent on imports of machinery, machine tools, instruments and project imports was introduced in March, 1995. Tariffs on imports of raw materials, manufactured intermediates and components for final goods have also been reduced by similar proportions. (For details, *see* Union Budget documents for 1991–92, 1992–93, 1993–94, 1994–95 and 1995–96). There was an explicit exchange rate depreciation in July, 1991 and an implicit exchange rate depreciation in March, 1992 when a dual exchange rate system was introduced and again in March, 1993 when the exchange rate was unified. Thus, between end-June, 1991 and end-June, 1993, in nominal terms, the rupee depreciated by 50 per cent *vis-a-vis* the US dollar. (For details, *see* Reserve Bank of India, *Annual Reports*).

53 See Government of India (1991a). For details of subsequent and related changes in this policy regime, *see* also Nayyar (1993b).

54 In September 1992, the government announced that pension funds and mutual funds from abroad would be allowed to invest in the domestic capital market subject simply to registration with the Securities and Exchange Board of India. The income tax rate on dividends from such portfolio investment has been fixed at 20 per cent for foreign institutional investors, which is much lower than the corporate income tax rate for domestic or foreign firms. The tax rates on long-term capital gains and short-term capital gains on such portfolio investment have been reduced from 40 per cent to 10 per cent and 30 per cent respectively, which are, once again, lower than what is payable by resident taxpayers. Foreign institutional investors are allowed to repatriate the principal, the capital gains, the dividends and any other receipt from the sale of such equity without any restriction at the market exchange rate. For details, *see* Government of India (1993) and Nayyar (1993b).

55 See, for example, Cooper in Corbo, Goldstein and Khan (1987), pp. 516–23.

56 The literature on this subject is vast. *See*, for example, Pack and Westphal (1986) and Dahlman, Ross-Larson and Westphal (1987). This argument is also developed further in Nayyar (1993a).

57 For details, see Government of India (1991a) and (1993).

58 For the evidence on disinvestment by the government and on non-plan budget support for the public sector cited in this paragraph, *see* Union Budget documents.

59 The elements of financial sector reform outlined in this paragraph are reported in the following documents : Reserve Bank of India, *Annual Reports* ; Economic Ministry of Finance, *Survey* ; Union Budget documents and Government of India (1993). *See* also Nayyar (1993b).

60 See Amsden (1989) and Wade (1991).

61 See Lall (1990), Stiglitz et al. (1989), Killick (1990) and Shapiro and Taylor (1990).

62 See Dahlman et al. (1987), Amsden (1989), Shapiro and Taylor (1990) and Wade (1991). *See* also World Bank (1993) and Singh (1994).

63 See Stiglitz (1989) and Krueger (1990).

64 For a detailed discussion, see Nayyar and Sen (1994). See also Bhalla (1994).

65 The simultaneous pursuit of macro-economic stabilization and structural reform—which is based on the orthodoxy of multilateral financial institutions—often compounds difficulties. In a situation of deep macro-economic disequilibrium, stabilization must restore a semblance of equilibrium in the economy before policy reform is used to restructure the economy. For discussion of this issue see Nayyar (1993a).

References

Amsden, A. (1989), *Asia's Next Giant : South Korea and Late Industrialization,* Oxford University Press, New York.

Bhagwati, J. and Desai, P. (1970). *India : Planning for Industrialization,* Oxford University Press, London.

Bhagwati, J. and Srinivasan, T.N. (1975). *Foreign Trade Regimes and Economic Development : India,* Columbia University Press, New York.

Bhagwati, J. and Srinivasan, T.N. (1993). *Indian Economic Reforms,* Ministry of Finance, New Delhi, July.

Bhalla, G. S. ed. (1994). *Economic Liberalization and Indian Agriculture,* ISID–FAO, New Delhi.

Cooper, R. N. (1992). *Economic Stabilization and Debt in Developing Countries,* The MIT Press, Cambridge.

Corbo, V., Goldstein, M. and Khan, M. ed. (1987). *Growth Oriented Adjustment Programs,* International Monetary Fund and The World Bank, Washington DC.

Cornia, G., Jolly, R. and Stewart, F. (1987). *Adjustment with a Human Face,* Clarendon Press, Oxford.

Dahlman, C., Ross-Larson, B. and Westphal, L. (1987). 'Managing Technological Development : Lessons from Newly Industrializing Countries', *World Development,* pp. 759–75.

Government of India (1991 a). *Statement on Industrial Policy,* Ministry of Industry, New Delhi, 24 July.

——— (1991b). *Statement on Trade Policy,* Ministry of Commerce, New Delhi, 13 August.

——— (1993). *Economic Reforms : Two Years After and the Task Ahead,* Ministry of Finance, New Delhi, June.

Griffin, K. B. (1970). 'Foreign Capital, Domestic Savings and Economic Development', *Bulletin of the Oxford University Institute of Economics and Statistics,* pp. 99–112.

Gupta, S. P. (1994). 'Recent Economic Reforms and their Impact on the Poor and Vulnerable Sections of the Society', *mimeo* ICRIER, New Delhi, November.

Killick, T. (1984). *The Quest for Economic Stabilisation : The IMF and the Third World,* Overseas Development Institute, London.

——— (1990). *A Reaction Too Far : Economic Theory and the Role of the State in Developing Countries,* Overseas Development Institute, London.

Krueger, A.O. (1990). 'Government Failures in Development', *Journal of Economic Perspectives,* pp. 9–23.

Krugman, P. and Taylor, L. (1978). 'Contractionary Effect of Devaluation', *Journal of International Economics,* pp. 445–56.

Lall, S. (1990). *Building Industrial Competitiveness in Developing Countries,* OECD Development Centre, Paris.

Nayyar, D. (1988). 'India's Export Performance : Underlying Factors and Constraints', in R.E.B. Lucas and G. F. Papanek, ed. *The Indian Economy : Recent Development and Future Prospects,* Westview Press, Boulder.

——— (1993a). *The Indian Economy at Crossroads : Illusions and Realities,* Frontier Lecture, Indian Institute of Science, Bangalore.

——— (1993b). 'Economic Reforms in India : A Critical Assessment', *ARTEP Working Paper,* ILO, New Delhi.

——— (1994a). 'The Foreign Trade Sector, Planning and Industrialization in India', in T.J. Byres. ed. *The State and Development Planning in India,* Oxford University Press, Delhi.

——— (1994b). *Migration, Remittances and Capital Flows : The Indian Experience,* Oxford University Press, Delhi.

Nayyar, D. and Sen, A. (1994). 'International Trade and the Agricultural Sector in India', in G. S. Bhalla. ed. *Economic Liberalization and Indian Agriculture,* ISID–FAO, New Delhi.

Pack, H. and Westphal, L. (1986). 'Industrial Strategy and Technological Change : Theory versus Reality', *Journal of Development Economics,* pp. 87–128.

Papola, T. S. (1993). 'Employment Growth and Social Protection of Labour in India', paper presented at the Round Table on 'Social Policy and Economic Liberalization : Contrasting Brazilian and Indian Experience and Strategies,' Sao Paulo, October.

Planning Commission. (1990). *Employment : Past Trends and Prospects for the 1990s,* Government of India, New Delhi.

——— (1993). *Report of the Expert Group on Estimation of Proportion and Number of Poor,* Government of India, New Delhi.

Shapiro, H. and Taylor, L. (1990). 'The State and Industrial Strategy', *World Development,* pp. 861–78.

Singh, A. (1994). 'Openness and the Market Friendly Approach to Development : Learning the Right Lessons from Development Experience', *World Development,* pp. 1811–24.

Stiglitz, J.E. et al. (1989). *The Economic Role of the State,* Basil Blackwell, Oxford.

——— (1989). 'Markets, Market Failures and Development', *American Economic Review, Papers and Proceedings*, pp.197–202.

Taylor, L. (1988). *Varieties of Stabilization Experience : Towards Sensible Macroeconomics in the Third World*, Clarendon Press, Oxford.

——— (1993). ed. *The Rocky Road to Reform : Adjustment, Income Distribution and Growth in the Developing World*, The MIT Press, Cambridge.

Wade, R. (1991). *Governing the Market*, Princeton University Press, Princeton.

Weisskopf, T. (1972). 'Impact of Foreign Capital Inflows on Domestic Savings in Underdeveloped Countries', *Journal of International Economics*, pp.25–38.

Williamson, J. (1983). ed. *IMF Conditionality*, Institute of International Economics, Washington DC.

Williamson, J. (1990). ed. *Latin American Adjustment : How Much Has Happened ?* Institute for International Economics, Washington DC.

World Bank. (1993). *The East Asian Miracle : Economic Growth and Policy*, Washington DC.